Active Sex after Sixty

Herman H. Rubin. M.D.
and
Benjamin W. Newman

New York

Published by ARCO PUBLISHING COMPANY, Inc.
219 Park Avenue South, New York, N. Y. 10003
Copyright © Herman H. Rubin & Benjamin W. Newman, 1969
All Rights Reserved
*No part of this book may be reproduced, by any means,
without permission in writing from the publisher, except
by a reviewer who wishes to quote brief excerpts in connection
with a review in a magazine or newspaper.*
Library of Congress Catalog Card Number 72-86900
Standard Book Number 668-01776-7
Printed in the United States of America

Contents

1. Look Forward to Continuing Sexual Joy 5
2. The Prelude to Intercourse 9
3. The Art of Love Play 12
4. Banish Taboos From Your Bedroom 18
5. The Sex Organs of Man 31
6. The Sex Organs of Woman 40
7. The Sex Life of Women Over 60 45
8. The Sex Life of Men Over 60 49
9. When Men Over 60 Marry 56
10. Can You Turn Back the Hands of Time? 61
11. The Role of Endocrine Glands in Sex 73
12. Mental Blocks to Successful Sex 85
13. Food For Sex Happiness 93
14. Sex and the Overweight 110
15. Are You "Too Tired" for Sex? 117
16. How to Attract a Mate 122

1. Look Forward to Continuing Sexual Joy

WE CHANGE IN ORDER to adjust to life from the day we are born! All through our lives, day after day, we must make adjustment both to external conditions and to internal conditions—to the weather, to the environment, to our day-by-day state of health, to our tensions and emotions. We must constantly make a hundred and one modifications and qualifications. As we grow older additional factors emerge to which we must adapt ourselves. We must regulate our activities in order to meet stress and strain so that fatigue does not become a major factor in our lives. Nutrition becomes more important. Relaxation and recreation become more necessary. And we must adjust our sexual activities.

Everyone looks for happiness in his or her own special way. But everyone needs a good physical body that functions properly—with vitality and energy—for psychological well-being. With this combination an active sex life can continue despite the rapid ticking away of time.

Since 1880 life expectancy has increased by thirty-five years. Now we can look forward to seventy years of life. But nobody wants merely to exist three-hundred-and-sixty-five-days a year.

Everybody wants a healthy, vigorous, and productive life through the long span of years. The exercise of common sense can make the difference!

The ability to conquer inhibitions and feelings of inadequacy will aid our physical bodies in countless ways to meet the complex demands of our civilized times. Inhibitions about sex and fears about age are heightened by the flood of material printed in newspapers and magazines extolling the role of youth. This becomes a challenge to the older members of our population. To rise above this unending barrage requires mental and emotional fortitude. Psychological conditions contribute mightily to sexual performance. Being worried, apprehensive, angry, or apathetic is not conducive either to the prolongation of sex life or to the prolongation of life itself.

This era is called the *Enlightened Age* or the *Scientific Age*! Scientific, yes! Children read books about guided missiles and spaceships. They take television trips to the moon and under the sea. They understand the principles of scientific wonders. Enlightened, possibly! Many taboos, false ideas, and prejudices have been exposed, are no longer believed, and are nearly forgotten. True, there has been a complete revolution of thought. What was whispered some years ago is now discussed openly. Yet in this presumably enlightened age it seems inconceivable that so many adults enter sex life with so little knowledge of the physiology of sex and with no acquaintance of the psychological mechanisms involved. Yet this is often true even of older men and women, many of whom have only a vague idea of how the sex act should be performed, of what happens to the physical body, and of the emotions before, during, and after coitus.

Is sex after sixty necessary? We believe it is! Sex life is a component of life itself—without it life is incomplete. Sex has always played an important role in art, music, literature, and in science; a sexless civilization could not exist.

The basic function of the sex drive in all animals is to ensure the perpetuation of the species. But there is a fundamental difference that sets apart the human animal from all others—including our closest primate relatives. In apes and monkeys, the female is sexually receptive only when she is in heat, at the time she is fertile. The human female is sexually receptive at any time of her reproductive cycle—whether or not she is fertile—and her sex life does not end when she is no longer able to conceive. On the contrary, there is often an increased desire for sexual gratification that only waits proper stimulation! When she is freed from the fear of unwanted pregnancy, a woman may experience the greatest sexual joy she has known in her life.

Evolutionists have speculated that the human female's sexual response is an evolutionary advance over mating behavior in other primates. Indeed, it is considered by many to have made human society possible. Among apes and monkeys, sexually mature males are constantly warring with each other for possession of the few females in heat at the moment. Constant availability of sexual gratification for the male is believed to have opened the doors to cooperation between men.

This book is dedicated to the normally sexed man or woman of sixty and over. The man is one whose appreciation of woman has grown through the years, who is always surprised by their reactions, who can never fully "understand" them, who never stops probing into their nature, and, finally, is a man whose desire for a woman has remained at a high level! The woman is one whose thoughts center about the love of a man, not any man but the special man she wants to be with in bed and out of bed, whom she wants to touch, to fondle, who wants to make her man happy in all things. She is the woman who has a sparkle in her eyes, who attracts men by her vivacity, her intelligence, and her health—she radiates vibrant life.

This book is written primarily for the layman. It contains many hints, plans, outlines, suggestions, ideas, instructions, and information that the authors have gathered from many authoritative sources. *Active Sex Over Sixty* is not only for the man and woman over sixty, but for those in their thirties, forties, and fifties who look forward to continuing sexual joy and fulfillment throughout their lives.

2. The Prelude to Intercourse

OUR CONCERN HERE is when the two sexes meet. Not merely to speak, or to eat together, or to see a play or movie together; but to engage in sexual activity that leads to sexual intercourse. It must be presumed that this pastime is nothing new. The man and woman are mature, they have practiced many times previously, usually while married, or possibly when single as a widow or widower or as a bachelor or bachelor girl with modern ideas.

There are reasons why everyone does not marry—financial obligations, not finding a compatible mate, having an ideal that cannot be met, or simply preferring single independence. It is a personal decision for the unmarried individual whether he wishes to enjoy sex or to live celibately. While waiting for the ideal partner, the days and years may rush by.

The man who in his youth wanted a five-foot-two brunette with eyes like liquid pools eventually may come to realize that he will never find her. He may now tremble in the knees when he is near a woman with beautiful gray hair. He usually is no longer looking for a woman to bear children in his image. What he now wants is a partner who will be solicitous when he is not feeling "100 percent," and who will be gay, amusing, and animated in bed. Not that a man makes concessions at this stage of life, but he has matured and come to realize that it is not the outside shell that is important.

A woman also matures. Her ideal—maybe some movie hero or perhaps some successful business figure—will slowly change. Not that she has lowered her standards, but intuition tells her that glamour and financial success are not essential attributes. She now may want gentleness and kindness in her mate.

Compatible partners are understanding partners. Sexual compatibility does not automatically come with marriage. Tiny details, a word or laugh at the wrong time may spoil an experience for the man or the woman. The wise wife will not criticize her husband's technique; she knows that one uncomplimentary word might make him unable to continue. A husband must show his tenderness, be unselfish, not commence the act too soon, be able to wait for her to be completely aroused and to have her orgasm with his or before his.

Total compatibility cannot be found in a "one-shot" affair. It takes patience for a couple to time their actions for complete sexual satisfaction. Both partners must learn which kisses and caresses are most stimulating and pleasurable to each other. This cannot be learned in one night!

Truly compatible couples do not discuss the sexual experiences they may have had with other partners. While making love they do not make sarcastic remarks, engage in political discussions, or talk about relations, friends, or anyone else but themselves. Each values the individuality of the other and is able to communicate this feeling.

Without a doubt every man and woman is more attracted to certain types of the opposite sex. Individual preferences are the result of previous experiences and personal inclinations. There are many who are immediately attracted sexually. However, two people who may initially be only somewhat attracted to each other can later develop sexual feelings and desires for each other.

What starts the chain of events that ends with intercourse? In partners of long standing often just one look, one word, or one brief gesture is all that is necessary to communicate desire. Sometimes there is no real preparation—some couples seem to view sex as something to be gotten over with so they can go to sleep. They neglect all the art; they always choose the same time. Why not try it in the afternoon, or before supper, or in the morning, have cocktails together at home after a show, and do the things that awaken anticipation? Why go to bed at exactly the same time? How about two-thirty in the morning when the rest of the world is asleep? This alone can give a romantic impetus.

In the prelude to intercourse four of our senses are involved. First, there is sight—just seeing his wife in a negligee, in an evening gown, or watching her walk, bend over, or even wash herself is often all the man needs. A woman may be aroused by the sight of her husband standing before a mirror nude, or flexing his arm muscles, even pulling in his stomach. Second, there is the sense of hearing—singing, talking, or listening to music may stir the emotions. Third there is smell—the natural smell of the body excites many, or the odor of perfume can work wonders in arousing desire. Fourth—and most important—there is the sense of touch—the squeeze of a hand or the pressure of a head against a shoulder.

3. The Art of Love Play

FANNING THE SPARK of passion into a powerful flame is an art in itself. The art of love play forms the basis of sexual happiness. But it is often neglected. The presumption that the mature man or woman knows all the answers is refuted by the multitudes of unsatisfied men and women who go through the sex act in a perfunctory manner as a duty to be performed. With this attitude the act is indulged less and less often until finally it may be abandoned through sheer boredom. To the artist in sex relations there is always much to discover that is new and exciting!

The nerve center that controls and coordinates changes in the sex organs and the rest of the body during sexual excitement and orgasm is located in the lower part of the spinal cord, in both men and women. This sex center may be stimulated by two pathways: Messages may pass down the spinal cord from the brain; or they may go directly to the lower spine through nerves from the genitals. Sensations arising from erogenous zones of the body (parts of the body most richly supplied with sensory nerve endings that respond to touch, such as the lips, breasts, thighs, and neck—or even from thoughts about a loved one—are relayed by the brain to the sex center. Nerves leaving this center connect with the sex organs, which become tumescent during excitement. The man's penis becomes erect; the woman's clitoris swells, and secretions from her vagina and labia start to flow.

Messages from the excited genitals travel up through the spinal cord to the conscious center of the brain, which experiences pleasure. The brain can send *inhibiting* messages back to the spinal center to limit the sexual response. This mechanism enables the man to control and delay his orgasm; it also, unfortunately, permits fears, anxiety, and tension to interfere with performance, resulting in impotence in the man or frigidity in the woman. Understanding of the miraculous function of the nervous system in the sex act can help overcome problems and gain maxium sexual pleasure.

Every man and woman has certain erogenous zones that are most sensitive to kissing and stroking. Experimentation will uncover these areas. For some, kissing of the eyes can be the height of sexual pleasure, though for most it is merely a sign of love. It has been reported that orgasm has occurred when a man kissed the eyelids of a woman, at the same time touching them with the tip of his tongue.

The actual touching of the genitals must be gentle. Here again, the partners will learn through experience how much pressure to apply. Some people enjoy vigorous touching, but most men and women enjoy gentle, soft, tender action.

The wife should be careful when she fondles her husband's testicles. It is just possible that in previous years she used too much strength, causing pain. She can erase such a memory by touching with extreme gentleness and can thus improve sexual relations. To import extreme pleasure, the wife should begin by lightly touching the back of the scrotum with the tips of her fingers, then continuing the same gentle touch around the testicles, finally bringing the finger tips along the penis to the tip. This is the method that is most effective in penile stimulation. The husband can be brought nearly to the point of orgasm, to control himself he must push his wife's hand away. After excitement subsides somewhat she can start all over again. She can continue this for some time while her husband caresses her.

Simultaneous excitement of the erogenous zones greatly arouses both man and woman. The husband can touch his wife's genitals while he is also kissing and fondling her breasts. The wife can caress her mate's genitals while she is kissing him in some other erogenous area, perhaps the lips.

Men are usually easily aroused unless very tired or lacking in virility. If the wife is to experience orgasm, manipulation of her genitals is nearly always necessary. The mature man knows that usually it takes a longer period of time at this age level.

During the love-play period the most sensitive part of the body in the vast majority of women is the clitoris. The male must titillate the woman's sexual organs for some time before intromission is attempted. Even the husband of many years seldom realizes that he must prepare his wife if there is to be a successful union. Learn how to employ love play effectively.

Excitement from her husband's caresses will cause the woman's thighs to separate, revealing the clitoris and the inner lips. The clitoris, excited by this love play, is enlarged, it is in erection. The husband will have no difficulty in locating it with his finger. Touching the lower side intensifies the wife's desire to a high degree.

When the husband excites the clitoris he should also caress the inner lips and the areas around it. The husband of long standing often fails to do this—the one thing he should not disregard—titillate the clitoris and also caress the inner lips and adjacent parts.

What other pleasurable preliminaries are there so that the couple may experience the highest mutual joy? Without any physical contact, without even touching or holding hands, there can be powerful physical reactions. Words of love or inviting glances can quicken the heartbeat and swell the erectile tissues. A wise spouse will know what to say, how to look at his or her mate, and will notice the result. Sometimes this will lead to

The Art of Love Play / 15

immediate intercourse when either one is easily aroused by some trifling action. The slower approach is much more satisfying.

Some wives instinctively know when to play the coquette. Many husbands like it and look forward to it. The woman makes an advance and then when she secures the attention of her husband she quickly withdraws; when he pursues she goes on the defensive. This teasing can sharpen the man's ardor, while the wife feels that she has made a conquest. The spirit of youth returns! Women want to be pursued, men want to be led and enticed! By coquetry a woman can induce her man to pay her compliments and tell her how much he loves her. Excitement and a feeling of closeness leads them to greater physical intimacy.

Many a man has said, "Let me kiss her just once and she is mine!" But it is rare indeed that a single kiss provides a magic "open sesame." However, there is a modicum of truth in the cliche. A couple may meet, come to know each other, and perhaps engage in a fleeting kiss as casual as a handshake; then later their first deep kiss can become the first step to physical intercourse. This applies to mature people as much as to the young. A kiss involves a very erogenous zone, and the sense of touch is the one most important to arousing desire.

For the couple in their sixties and over, the deeply felt kiss between man and wife is a powerful stimulant. So few employ the kiss for this purpose; so few know how to kiss; so few try various kissing techniques. A brief pressing of the lips is the usual kiss—there is no fervor behind it. Each kiss should be different, the approach different, the action different—even if a hundred kisses are made in succession.

With a real love-mate the husband can pass his tongue along his wife's lips, left to right then right to left; he can press his tongue deeply into her mouth and she can reciprocate; he can enclose her mouth with his until there is a slight hurt which she finds pleasurable.

Open-mouth kissing can be a gentle or intense meeting of tongues, both partners press their lips together and then proceed with an in and out movement of the tongues, reaching for sensitive areas. If you have never tried these different kinds of kisses, discover them now. Even after long years of married life you can find new joy and erotic sensation.

In the most common type of kissing, lips closed pressed to closed lips, the sensation is mainly that of touching, whereas in the tongue kiss the sense of taste plays a part also. The tongue exploring the mouth brings taste and touch together for this supreme type of fervent kiss. Taste plays a part also in the suction kiss, another kiss that yields much pleasure. With this variety of kisses the artists of love have a full palate of colors—they can combine them in a infinite number of ways: They can kiss various parts of the body, the eyes, the neck, the shoulders. and—for the woman—the breasts most of all!

Many women enjoy and encourage breast kissing. A woman will present her breasts to her mate, inviting him to kiss them. The wife need not say a word, her actions speak for themselves. The husband can employ either the suction kiss or the tongue kiss around the breasts and nipples. This love play will arouse the wife to a high pitch of sexual excitement.

In many cases the various actions of the prelude and love play make the male partner too excited, and when he enters his wife he ejaculates quickly, leaving her unsatisfied or he may penetrate her before she is ready to receive him. It is the duty of the male to bring his wife to the peak of preparedness before he attempts intromission. As the male is ready much more quickly, he must perfect his art so that the wife will arrive at the peak of desire at the same time that he reaches this level. The art is for both partners to act in concert. It may take the woman a considerably longer time for all stages of love-making, but husband and wife must be ready for the act at the same time, the wife must not be cheated of her orgasm by a too hasty male.

Active love play has been described thus far. There is also *passive* love play. The passive contact of bodies alone can lead to coitus. Here both male and female do nothing. Their bodies touch and that is all. They may read; they may rest; they may remain passive for hours. All the time each is acutely aware of contact with the other's body. They may indulge in active foreplay for a while and then return to resting until the call for action comes, the call of desire leading to the sex act.

Many feel that there is something wrong in any kind of love play—their kisses contain little or no passion—they are frightened, not realizing the vital importance of love play, not knowing that it is fundamental to success in the paramount act of love.

4. Banish Taboos from Your Bedroom

Now is the time for enjoyment, time to experiment, time to do things you never ventured before. Now that you have matured emotionally, you and your partner must forget what your children or relations would say, what the neighbors would think. Banish taboos from your bedroom!

Try out the "high jinks" you have heard about, put to the test stories you have read about love in other parts of the world. Now there should be no inhibitions. You have perhaps retired or will soon retire from a full week's work; if you are a woman you are past the menopause. So why not experiment with lovemaking and experience love's final object? Now is the time to express feelings and desires. Be honest with each other, if there is some act you have repressed because of shyness, now is the time to bring it to the surface. Your partner will delight in sharing and trying the long hidden desire. This is no time to be timid, maximum response is now the goal. Make your preferences known, it might be only to try a different position or type of love play instead of the one practiced for years and years. You and your mate at this time of life can have supreme enjoyment that will bring you closer and closer together in all things. Sex must not become stale. Now is the time to bring intelligence and fresh ideas and fresh vigor to the activities in the bedroom!

Intercourse begins from the moment the male inserts his penis into the vagina. Now the two bodies merge into one—this complete physical union mirrors the emotional and spiritual union. Kissing and caressing should be continued during the actual sex act for full expression of feeling.

The wife is commonly thought to be the passive partner. Actually her organs are very active even if she appears to be in a passive role. Her heart beats more rapidly during this erotic excitement; her labial arteries pulsate strongly; her genital organs grow turgid and hot. Her vagina contracts and dilates until she reaches climax with complete gratification. She moves her body in response to the male, meeting every motion of her partner's with her own. The act of coitus is one of mutual cooperation. The pleasure of copulation is not localized in the genital organs but enjoyed by the entire body. Relief—orgasm—when it comes gives total satisfaction to the entire person.

Boredom in sex is a destructive force in a marriage. Boredom has usually set in by middle age because of a mechanical and repetitious sex life. This can be remedied by introducing variety and novelty. Both husband and wife must be interesting people who enjoy each other individually and who are interested in their sex life. Experimentation will break the routine of a sex relationship and bring new meaning to the union.

There are many positions for intercourse. Try them, modify and change them to suit your individual needs and tastes. Make release from sexual tension a pleasure and an inspiration! Then you and your partner will again be eager and anxious for sexual union.

Described here are various positions for intercourse. There are many, many more listed in erotic literature—in fact there are from one hundred to three hundred mentioned. However they are mostly variations from the basic positions, or are so ingenious and difficult that only a pair of acrobats or contortionists could manage them.

There are several guidelines that you should adhere to. Select positions of comfort. Do not attempt sexual tricks or acrobatics. If intercourse is between two thin persons, select the most comfortable position or positions. The same rule applies to coitus between a heavy man and a thin woman or a heavy woman and a thin man. Several positions for both fat men and fat women are listed in the chapter on obesity. If you have a coronary (heart) condition, consult your physician about frequency of intercourse. Do not indulge when fatigued or under great mental stress. Do not prolong the act to a point of exhaustion in order to satisfy your mate. If your mate does not arrive at climax during intercourse, manipulate the organ until orgasm is achieved. Some women after sixty have a tendency to dryness of the vagina which may make intercourse painful. Lubricate the penis thoroughly and then perform slowly and gently. Do not force the issue if either mate is asleep or tired, wait for a more opportune time. If you are impotent or partially impotent and still have a powerful sex urge you may both obtain satisfaction by manipulation.

The normal position (or habitual or fundamental) is with the wife on her back. It is also known as the "male dominant" position. The woman lies on her back, her thighs separated, her knees are slightly bent. The male lies upon his partner's abdomen and supports himself by his knees and elbows on the bed in order to relieve her of some of his weight. His legs and thighs are between hers. Small wonder this position is so popular, the two bodies make nearly complete contact. At the same time there can be much love play, the woman's hands are free to caress the man's buttocks, back, head and arms. The male can rest on one arm while caressing the woman. He can crouch down and fondle and kiss her breasts. Both can exchange kisses. The two bodies in this contact, from thighs to chest, gives a great range of emotion and sensation. The stimulation found in this normal position is of a moderate degree. One advantage of this position, it is suitable for the woman who reaches climax quickly. Penetration is not deep in this "normal" position—raising the woman's pelvis by placing pillows under her buttocks will make penetration deeper. For variety the woman can place her knees in the hollows of her partners knees. The woman can take an active part in this position because both her hands are free. The one disadvantage of this position concerns the ability of the male to control his climax. It is difficult for him to relax even if he stops all activity. Any movement of the woman can easily bring about orgasm, if he has reached that point. Only supreme control can retard it. Here the woman can greatly assist in prolonging the sex act. After having relations a few times she will know just how far to go—she can aid in achieving control in this position. The normal position usually results in synchronized movement by both partners, with the male as a rule, starting movement slowly then advancing to a rapid action with the woman following right along. If the act is to be stopped when approaching climax in order to extend the duration of pleasure and excitement, there must be complete self-control by both partners—complete suppression!

Another position with the woman on her back is suitable for the male who does not have a full erection. After the penis is inserted, she closes her thighs by stretching out her legs to their full length between the man's legs. Here her closed thighs hold the penis in the vagina even if it is not hard and firm. His thighs enclose and clasp hers. The friction of the penis against the female pelvis and against the inner portions of the woman's thighs will cause an increased erection throughout the length of the male organ. The woman will receive great pleasure as her clitoris and labia majora will be greatly excited. The man's enjoyment might not be as great, the lower part of his phallus might not come in contact with the vagina.

A third position begins with the woman lying on her back, the male being dominant. This position might be tried by thin agile persons. After intromission, the woman draws her knees up until they nearly reach her breasts, up to the man's shoulders if possible. A variation has the woman lift her legs at right angles to her body from her hips, then resting them on the shoulders of her mate who now inserts his phallus. In this position both parties receive extreme excitement and pleasure, the male because he has made deep penetration allowing for longer strokes, the woman because the deep penetration of the penis provides both clitoral and vaginal stimulation. The position with the woman's legs on the shoulders of the male cannot be attained by all women and should not be attempted if there is discomfort. A modification can give the same sensation. Here the woman lies on her back, opens her thighs as widely as possible and bends her knees. Intercourse in this position is just as pleasurable and more universally employed.

For a complete change there is the position where the husband and wife sit facing each other. The man is seated on a chair, stool, or on the edge of the bed, and the wife sits on his lap. He holds his knees apart, which allows him to open his partner's thighs. Full indulgence in love-play is possible with the hands being free. The wife controls all movements of her pelvis. The husband can pull his wife toward him by clasping her hips and thighs with his hands. Deep penetration is quite possible. In this position orgasm will not be of extreme intensity for either the man or woman.

Another position is where the wife lies on her belly and the man enters from behind. Successful coitus is only possible for slim, lean people. If the husband is corpulent to any appreciable degree or his wife is blessed with an ample buttock, this position becomes difficult, if not impossible. Conception is unlikely, the seminal fluid flows out quickly along the downward sloping passage toward the external orifice. Only the exceptional, experienced, very quickly responsive woman can have complete satisfaction in this position.

Side-by-side positions where the husband enters from behind

makes deep penetration quite impossible. Start with both partners lying on their left sides. This allows the male to embrace and clasp his wife, to stroke and caress her with his free right hand. If one has never tried this position, he might think it is quite impossible; however, it can easily be achieved: The wife draws up her right leg, opening her thighs slightly for the male to insert his penis; then she closes her thighs. The starting position can be reversed with both partners lying on their right sides. The excitations are sufficient for a weak climax in a passionate woman with a harmonious conjugal partner. For the male, side-by-side coitus supplies enough stimulation and sensation for ejaculation and relief. For both partners this position is the least exhausting method.

To supply freshness and a general lift of morale, a start is made by the wife lying on her back, her husband on top, the old time "normal" position. The woman brings her legs up to rest against her husbands flanks, the couple clasp each other tightly and roll over onto their sides. Now they are facing each other with their hands free for all manner of caresses, with all types of kissing bringing excitement to the experience. Movement is restricted so that there will be no loss of engagement. When they are approaching culmination, the couple can roll back so that the wife is again on her back. Through this action the sex act can be prolonged until both partners are near climax.

Kneeling positions are very popular with men and women who want to try something different. It is often the first change that enters their minds, they can think of no other. The wife takes a kneeling position so that her body, from trunk to thigh, is inclined at a more or less acute angle. The wife can stretch her body horizontally, supporting herself on her hands and arms or on her elbows. The husband kneels behind the wife, he can bend over so that he rests upon the almost horizontal back of his wife. For a variation, the wife, while standing, bends over a chair or divan with the husband behind her. This allows for deep penetration. Both partners to the act receive powerful sensations. The male can employ all methods of love play except mouth-to-mouth kissing.

There is another seated position. The male sits on a chair or stool and takes his partner on his lap with the woman's back toward him. Again her hands cannot be used for caressing. She cannot kiss her mate. These are disadvantages to be considered. Remember a woman's hands contain magic sensations for a man. The male can use his hands to titillate the woman's breasts or her clitoris. In this position there is the danger of the phallus slipping out during the movements of coitus. This will not happen if the wife seats herself far enough back on the lower portion of her husband's abdomen and tilts her pelvis down and toward her husband arching her back so that there is backward pressure on the vaginal entrance.

You will discover some positions that aid the wife to climax, some positions that offer more opportunities for kisses and caresses during coitus. The wife has more freedom of movement when she is on top of her husband, particularly if he is much heavier and larger than she. In the side-by-side position there is less tension for the husband. The prime objective always is mutual gratification.

With this number of positions possible it is deplorable that so many couples adopt just one and stick to it rigidly. Through variety each individual's preferences will be met. Experimentation in sexual intercourse is never immoral or degrading. Quite the opposite is true: When men and women free themselves from false morality, marital happiness will be their lot. Use every organ of the body for pleasure and gratification. Discover complete freedom sexually. (The only limitations are activities that cause discomfort.)

Many women go through their entire lives without ever experiencing orgasm. They do not know what it is. For centuries writers have tried unsuccessfully to describe this sensation in which the entire body and mind participate.

Intercourse is directed toward orgasm (ejaculation) by the man and orgasm of the woman. The man's ejaculation will sometimes bring on the woman's orgasm: A few moments before his orgasm, the man's body is so gripped by the reproductive instinct that he has little or no control over his thrusting motions. This action results in the expulsion of semen in a series of rhythmic spasms, which excite the woman to her own climax. Orgasm in the woman is a paroxysm of muscular movements in her vagina and throughout her body.

The male receives complete release from the previous sexual stimulation—an immediate sense of calm and tranquility follows. With the woman there is a period of time after orgasm in which excitement slowly subsides. A woman may sometimes experience a continuous orgasm, a long spasm or a series of shorter bursts resembling the ejaculation of the male, that leaves a feeling of euphoria and deep relaxation.

Recent research work has exploded many theories about human sexuality. For years sexologists talked about the distinction between clitoral and vaginal orgasms in women, but Masters and Johnson have shown that the physiological reactions of the body during orgasm are the same, no matter what type of stimulation is employed to trigger the climax. Another long-cherished fallacy was that a woman always takes a longer time to reach the point of orgasm than a man. But it has been demonstrated that women can achieve orgasm in a minute or two through masturbation. When not properly aroused by her mate, however, a woman comes to climax slowly, if at all. A particularly encouraging discovery is that men of advanced age are capable of ejaculation. *Even at eighty years or more men are able to emit semen.*

A popular misconception that can lead to marital discord at all age levels concerns simultaneous orgasm by husband and wife. Why this becomes so important is difficult to understand. An older man may be dismayed when he cannot bring his wife to orgasm exactly when he is ready. Many a wife tries to "hurry up," thereby missing many of the joys of intercourse. Simultaneous climax can occur if the couple employs sufficient will power; however, when this is the main object there is less pleasure in the act. Far better for both to completely immerse themselves in the act. Should the man have his orgasm first, he can still bring his wife to orgasm by various methods. If the wife is first she can wait for her husband while she uses all the arts of love play. Striving for simultaneous orgasm can lead to impotence in the man and frigidity in the woman, with the woman sometimes feigning orgasm in order to please her husband.

Withdrawal by the man without ejaculation is almost universally condemned by physicians. Incomplete sexual intercourse can be the cause of nervous disorders and hysteria. When complete normal sex relations are resumed health is soon regained. There are two methods that have been used to prevent deposition of sperm in the vagina: *coitus reservatus,* where ejaculation is prevented by prolonging intercourse until the erection of the penis (still in the vagina) subsides; and *coitus interruptus,* where the penis is withdrawn just before orgasm and ejaculation occurs when the penis is outside the woman's body or ejaculation is completely suppressed. *Coitus reservatus* was practiced by a group calling themselves the "Society of Perfectionists." Founded by Humphrey Noys in New York State in the early decades of the nineteenth century, the society members believed that the male could be assured a full sex life until old age if he conserved his seminal fluid for reabsorption by his body. (Of course there was no way to prevent the accumulated semen from leaving the body through nocturnal emissions or in the process of urination.) The Society of Perfectionists did not flourish— their men and women were too unsatisfied!

The more subtle movements of intercourse that produce exquisite sensations are often neglected, perhaps because they are unknown or because orgasm comes too quickly to allow sufficient time. A rotary motion of the pelvis provides greater stimulation to the clitoris of the woman and the glands of the man than the straight thrust. Since this circular motion requires control over many muscles, the wife of mature years needs to practice this with patience. She does not have to become a belly dancer, she should just develop enough flexibility to be able to slowly rotate her hips for added enjoyment. There is a ring of muscle, called the vaginal sphincter, in the vaginal wall just inside the passage opening. It is possible for a woman to learn to contract and relax this muscle at will. Tightening this muscle will enable a woman to help her mate maintain a full erection, thereby increasing her own pleasure. Rhythmic contraction and relaxation of the vaginal sphincter can also enhance the sensations of intercourse for both man and wife by providing variations in pressure on sensitive tissues. Various strokes and rhythms also may be employed, and teasing techniques may possibly be brought into play.

Some primitive races and Oriental people believe that a circumsized male is better able to prolong the act of intercourse than an uncircumsized male. It would appear, however, that the ability to prevent early ejaculation is mainly a matter of control and experience. If the husband has a quick orgasm he can, after a short rest, make a second intromission. Usually this second contact will last much longer so that the wife will arrive at a satisfactory orgasm.

There is little doubt that normal sexual intercourse produces a certain amount of lassitude, a desire for rest. Is this the time for a husband to turn his back on his wife and promptly fall asleep? No! Even after a long marriage it is still a shock to a wife that when orgasm has occurred her husband seems to lose all interest in her. This can give her a feeling that he is an infant who, after being fed (intercourse), is overcome by sleep. Or a wife can think that her husband only desires her body—that once his need is gratified he wants to go his own way. She can be deeply wounded by his actions, and much harm can be done to the relationship.

For the couple sixty or over there might be a longer period of preparation for the act. This will not be a hit-and-run affair, but a communion. It will occur between lovers whose souls and bodies share in the rapture, intensely, and with delicacy.

Remembering that it takes his wife longer to become aroused, the man should realize that her ecstasy will last longer, that it takes her longer to return to normal. Few men seem to understand that a woman experiences a slow decrescendo of sexual excitement. The husband enjoyed the period of love play, he was all tenderness, so now he should enter the period of the afterglow with equal anticipation if he wants to contribute to his wife's sexual felicity.

With the completion of the sexual act the husband should embrace his wife, kiss her, hold her in his arms, give her a feeling of being wanted, impart to her a sense of security, reveal to her that he wanted her because of his love for her. Then they can rest side by side, giving nature a little time to restore them. During this time of drowsy relaxation they can relive the experience in imagination.

The slow return can be enhanced by drinking or eating, by conversation, by listening to music—to deepen their communication with one another. This after-glow should be allowed to continue—there is no time limit until there might be a nap for both or even a return to more love play, perhaps even to a second act of coitus. The husband shows his gratitude, the wife her gratification. There is then the memory of the occasion, the hope for a repetition.

After sexual communion there comes the most exquisite happiness—mental and physical peace! Then comes sleep in each others' arms and the wife is able to express her maternal instinct to the man sleeping on her breast. Afterplay is one of the most significant acts in the love drama!

Science has exploded the erroneous concepts that masturbation is harmful, that it in some mysterious manner comes between husband and wife in their marriage partnership, and that it is only indulged by children and adolescents! But, despite scientific facts, innumerable misconceptions and prohibitions still conceal the role of masturbation in our society. Few in the past would even talk about this subject—it was not discussed in print. The few who had the daring were quickly suppressed and censored. These distortions at one time or another claimed that this behavior bought on every kind of illness known to man. In early times masturbation was penalized by death. In the 1800s masturbation was blamed for all the major ailments including insanity. This insanity fable in the list of modern myths about autoeroticism is still with us. The other myths about epilepsy, cancer and sterility have gradually faded away.

Masturbation is part of marriage. There are times in marriage when each of the partners resorts to this practice—during menstruation, during a long separation, before delivery of a child, and during times when one partner has been stimulated to a high degree. In the marriage state masturbation can safeguard the happiness of both partners. It is a constructive activity —the balance wheel when there is unequal desire between man and wife.

For the unmarried adult it can be a sexual outlet, a means for the release of tension. Women masturbate when they are unable to climax during intercourse—when they have not been aroused sufficiently by love play, or when their partner leaves them high and dry by being inconsiderate. Often there is a consuming desire by the single man or woman to masturbate for sexual release when a partner is not available. All experts concur that it is a perfectly valid outlet for gratification in this period of great stress.

In the early years of marriage about 40 percent of the husbands resort to masturbation at times. This trend decreases until at ages fifty to fifty-five only about 10 percent indulge. This may be due to a more complete adjustment of the marriage partners or to other variables. In a survey of men over sixty-five, fully 25 percent engaged in this practice. In a study of a small group of widows aged sixty to eighty, all found release from sexual desire in masturbation. There is on record a man who daily masturbated at age sixty-five.

5. The Sex Organs of Man

UNTIL RECENT TIMES THE function of the sex glands was thought to be only reproductive. Their role as glands of internal secretion was unknown.

A normal, happy existence is impossible unless the gonads function correctly. Upon their secretions depends our vigor for the tasks of everyday life, our ability to think clearly, the fulfillment of our most intimate desires and, above all, our morale. The health of the gonads determines our capacity for wholesome relationships with our mates, our offspring, our associates in business and social life, indeed with humanity in general. People deficient in sex secretions are apt to be equally short of affection and sympathy. A good society can be built only on the foundation of a normal, energetic, sexually adequate people.

The ovaries in a woman are often said to be the equivalent of the testicles of man. This is hardly correct. There is an important difference between the ovaries and the testicles. In the female the ovaries produce both eggs and hormones but one does not occur without the other—they work together in unison! However, in the male, the testicles show an entirely different action. Here the production of hormones has nothing to do with the production of the sperm cells. If, for some reason, sperm output fails in a man, he may still have normal sex impulses. The cells that produce the male hormone function independently from the cells that produce the spermatozoa.

For each mature ovum (egg) released by the female each lunar month, the male develops an estimated 850,000,000 sperm cells. An astronomical figure! Under the microscope egg cells appear much larger and do not move by themselves. The spermatozoa are quite active and propel themselves by their whiplash tails. The sperm cells are the smallest cells of the human body; the egg cells are the largest.

The testicles are suspended beneath the pelvis in a pouch called the scrotum that holds the two egg-shaped $1\frac{1}{2}$ ounce testicles. There is a most remarkable mechanism for keeping the testicles relatively cool, because, if they are too warm, this would prevent the development of normal sperm. A layer of muscle in the scrotum called the cremasteric muscle, raises or lowers the testicles to bring them closer to the warm body if they are too cool, or to let them hang farther down when they are warm. Sperm cannot be produced at a temperature as high as that of the abdominal cavity. Normally the testicles in the scrotum have a temperature slightly lower than the interior of the body. In cold weather they are pulled up closer to the body; in warmer weather the muscle relaxes so that the testicles drop downward away from the high body temperature.

Each testicle is about $1\frac{1}{2}$ to 2 inches in length and $\frac{3}{4}$ to 1 inch in width. In almost half of all adult males, one testicle, the left one, is suspended lower than its mate.

Each testicle is enveloped in an outer covering surrounded by membranes known as tunics. Inside each testicle is a series of *lobules* (compartments) that resemble sections in an orange. From the extreme depth of each lobule is a tube that extends to the outside. All of the tubes from all of the compartments unite to form the *epididymis*, a common tube that extends from the upper to the lower end of each testicle. The epididymis is folded back and forth upon itself then runs through the scrotum to the *seminal vesicles,* a pair of organs just under the bladder. It is now recognized that the seminal vesicles do not store spermatozoa, either living or dead, but do form a fluid that adds bulk to the seminal discharge.

The sperm are formed within microscopic twisted tubules in every lobule. These tubules would extend about 300 yards per teste if they were placed end to end. Sperm production is at work constantly in a healthy man—starting perhaps as early as eight years of age—every day of the year, ever second of every minute. There are no holidays, no coffee breaks, no time-and-a-half for overtime. The sperm factory is in operation whether it is hot or cold in every man all over the world.

Newly manufactured cells are passed through the epididymis by slow wavelike contractions of the tubules. The spermatozoa attain their physiological maturity during this passage and are carried into the *vas deferens,* the final conducting tube. Sperm only retain their vitality for a few days and then decline in vigor and finally die. If they are not ejaculated, the aged sperm degenerate in the vas deferens and are finally absorbed. There are times when ejaculations are too close together to allow the sperm time to mature in the epididymis.

With each emission some 200,000,000 sperm are expelled— for the more fertile man the figure is probably closer to 300,000,000! The odds against any particular sperm completing the hazardous journey to a meeting with the ova are very high. But it cannot be assumed that the hundreds of millions of sperm that fall by the wayside are wasted, because when the number of sperm per ejaculation falls below a minimum level— 60,000,000 is a commonly accepted minimum—the chances of effecting conception is practically nil. Enzymes released by sperm in the vicinity of the egg help the lucky one to penetrate the cell membrane. Obviously, the sperm that don't get to the egg serve some function.

So you see that it may sometimes be the fault of the male that a marriage does not produce babies. A man may be *potent* (able to perform sexual intercourse) and yet be *sterile* (unable to father a child). Male sterility may be due to factors other than insufficient sperm production: The spermatic duct may be obstructed; immotile or otherwise imperfect sperm may be produced. Sometimes a feeble constitution may be responsible for a decrease in the number of sperm and they may be too weak and ill-nourished to reach their uterine goal. Undoubtedly this weeding-out process works for the vigor of the species. In rare instances an individual is unable to produce any sperm at all.

The ejaculated fluid, called semen, contains a complicated mixture of secretions from the epididymis, vas deferens, seminal vesicles, and the prostate gland. The greater bulk of the fluid comes from the *prostate*, a chestnut-size gland that surrounds the urethra just below the bladder. Malfunction of any of the secretory organs can cause sterility, by depriving sperm of the proper medium in which to swim. The amount of semen discharged and its appearance and composition will vary in an individual according to his state of health, endocrine balance, diet, and frequency of coitus; and the same factors determine differences between individuals. Semen ranges in color from a pale white to a rather dark yellow; its consistency varies from that of egg albumin to heavy mucus. Repeating coitus in a short period of time will reduce the amount ejaculated; continence for a few days will increase the amount.

Recent research has shown that in about 40 percent of the infertile couples studied, it was the man who was responsible. Though these males manifested average sexual desire, genital development, body size and form, and hair distribution, their sperm counts were below the 60,000,000 level.

The man over sixty who marries a younger woman may find it difficult to believe that it may be his fault that there are no children, especially when his sexual desire is strong and his sex relations with his wife are satisfactory. A mature man in a childless marriage should see a doctor for a sperm count and a complete examination of the genital organs. Chemical tests may also be performed to determine the composition of the semen. It is then up to the man to follow through on treatment the doctor prescribes to correct his condition.

One cause of insufficient sperm production is a delay of the descent of one or both of the testicles from the abdominal cavity into the scrotum, which normally takes place during the third month of life—six months before the boy baby is born! In passing from the abdominal cavity, each of the testes makes a channel called the *inguinal canal* in muscles of the abdominal wall. (This channel sometimes in later life is a point of weakness at which a muscle strained by heavy lifting or even by constipation may rupture, forming an inguinal hernia.) As discussed earlier, sperm production may be carried on only at a certain temperature, which is below that of the abdominal cavity. If the testes do not descend on schedule to the scrotum where the temperature is cooler, irreparable harm may be done. The longer they remain at the higher temperature, the greater the deterioration of the sperm-producing tissue. An undescended testicle may be brought down by surgical means; when the surgery is too late, it remains sterile.

The penis consists of three cyclindrical-shaped masses of spongy erectile tissue bound together with connective tissues surrounded by a layer of skin. Under normal conditions these tissues are nearly empty of blood and are collapsed. During sexual excitement they fill with blood, enlarging and stiffening the penis. At erection the average penis is 6 inches in length, ranging in different individuals from $5\frac{1}{2}$ to $6\frac{1}{2}$ inches.

Dilation of the arteries of the penis is controlled by nerves from the lower end of the spinal cord. The nerves that control the discharge connect with the same spinal nerve center. Discharge is largely a reflex action initiated through the same impulses that brought about erection. At the time of ejection the spermatozoa are squeezed from the vas deferens into the urethra in the base of the penis; further volume is added by secretions from the prostate and seminal vesicles. The collected semen is then ejected by a muscle that squeezes down upon the urethra. After ejaculation the arteries that carry blood into the penis narrow down, the spongy tissues of the penis are drained of blood, and there is a collapse of the erection.

Here is complete coordination between the messages from the brain, spinal nerve impulse, muscle contraction, and blood flow. The physical and emotional factors controlling erection and orgasm are so interrelated that potency may be destroyed by failure at any point—whether there be a structural defect, a hormone deficiency, fatigue, poor health, disease of any part of the reproductive apparatus, sex fears and inhibitions, or general emotional tension. Impotence may also result from diseases such as syphilis, gonorrhea, or diabetes; from lesions of the brain and spinal cord; or it may follow almost any debilitating ailment. Drugs, alcohol, or even excessive smoking may be responsible. Obviously, older men do not have a monopoly on problems of impotence.

The prostate keeps growing until the age of twenty, then stops. It starts growing again after age fifty, continuing for ten to twenty years. It is believed that this second increase in size may be associated with sexual activity, because the second growth of the prostate is rare among the celibate clergy.

Recent studies have much to say about impotence. Only about 5 percent of all men are impotent at sixty years of age. This increases to 30 percent at seventy years of age. At age 75 the percentage of men who are impotent rises to 55. At ninety years of age there are still some potent men!

Zipporah, the wife of Moses, "Took a sharp stone and cut off the foreskin of her son." This is described in the Old Testament. The Jews were not the first to practice circumcision; there are records of this practice among primitive tribes. In ancient Egypt boys were generally circumcised between the ages of six and twelve. Among the Abyssinians, the Hebrews, the Mohammedans, and a few other people circumcision is performed shortly after birth. One of the earliest representations of the procedure is a series of pictures on the wall of an Egyptian tomb dating back to 2400 B.C. To the Hebrew, circumcision is both a religious rite and a hygenic measure. There is less syphilis among males that have been circumcised. The wives of Hebrews and Moslems have fewer cancers of the womb than other women.

There is no agreement on the effect of circumcision on the sexual act. A slight majority of researchers believe it heightens male gratification during sexual relations.

Castration has always been regarded as a major calamity for a man. Not only does it result in sterility, but also pronounced changes in personality occur. These changes in personality have been a source of wonder and speculation from ancient times.

Myths of Babylonia, of Phoenicia, and of other lands of long ago give accounts of men castrating themselves when in a religious frenzy. In Asia, castration has been a religious rite among several sects. Guardians of harems were nearly always castrated men, called *eunuchs*. The Sultans and Pashas protected their many wives in this way from being molested by men of the household. It was also common knowledge that the beautiful singing voices of boys could be conserved by castration. This practice was in vogue for some church choirs until 1870. For many years the soprano roles in the opera were sung by men who had been castrated when they were boys. Aristotle, in about 300 B.C., described the results of bird castration—in the mature birds the crest turned yellow and the bird lost its sexual passion and ability to crow. He also described castration of boys—their voices did not deepen, their public and facial hair failed to appear.

Eunuchism is a prevalent male sex disorder. If the testes are absent, so is sexual desire and potency. When the testes are present but notably underactive, a condition known as *eunuchidism* (like a eunuch) arises. Victims of either condition are nervous, excitable, and effeminate. They are also often dullwitted and sluggish or shy and unstable. For them life is extremely difficult.

Emasculation of an adult may be the result of an accident. Sometimes surgical removal of the testes is necessary when there is a cancerous growth or some other disease of the testicles. The adult loses facial hair and shaving soon becomes unnecessary. The distribution of the pubic hair actually changes from that of the male to the transverse pattern of the female! There is a tendency toward obesity as sexual impulse and potency go into decline. The usual picture of the emasculated adult is that of a fat, tired old man.

From the known results of castration, it was believed that the source of a man's vitality must be in the testicles. No one suspected that these effects were due not to a depletion of sperm but the loss of some other substance produced in the testicles.

Histologist Franz von Leydig (1821–1908) was the first to describe the interstitial cells of the testicles that are known as the "cells of Leydig." He discovered these cells in the loose connective tissue surrounding the seminiferous tubules in which the sperm are formed.

The attempt to isolate and identify the substance produced by these cells was a long, exasperating and frustrating search. Scientists in all fields of medicine made extracts in every conceivable form and administered them both orally and by injection. It was not until 1927 that this substance was successfully isolated by organic chemist Professor Fred C. Koch of the University of Chicago. The first test on a human was on a twenty-six-year-old man, really a half man! This young man had little pubic hair; his voice was childish; he was without sexual sensations; and he had never discharged sperm. Injections were made for fifty-three days. Soon he began to feel the urge of sexual desire, he became sexually strong and normal. For the first time in his life he ejaculated semen.

Soon a synthetic method was found to manufacture this male hormone, now called *testosterone*. Testosterone, which is secreted directly into the blood stream by the cells of Leydig, is a muscle builder as well as a regulator of sexual desire. It has important effects upon tissue growth and development of male characteristics. Administration of testosterone has been prescribed with good results for improvements of muscular strength, endurance, and recovery from fatigue, as well as for treatment of impotence, eunuchism, and eunuchoidism. Certain nervous conditions such as restlessness, anxiety, insomnia, and the inability to concentrate have also been relieved by testosterone therapy.

Although the hormone is necessary for normal male maturation, the degree of development of the deep male voice, body and facial hair, and heavy musculature are not solely determined by the amount of testosterone produced. Heredity plays an important part, and there is wide variation in these characteristics among normal, virile males. In other words, exceptional hairiness, an unusually deep voice, and extraordinary muscular development does not mean that a man is "more male," nor does scant hair growth, a lighter voice, and a slight build necessarily make a man "less male."

It is, however, much easier to diagnose testosterone deficiency than it is to detect overproduction of the hormone, because there is a point in the continuum where characteristics become decidedly effeminate. This is not true at the other end of the scale —it cannot be determined from physical appearance whether or not a man is "too male." But overactivity of the cells of Leydig can cause as much trouble as underactivity. Violent behavior and uncontrollable sex urges may be symptoms of this condition.

6. The Sex Organs of Woman

LIKE THE TESTICLES OF the man, the ovaries of a woman come in a pair—bean-shaped organs about an 1½ inches long and about 1 inch wide. They are located in the pelvis, suspended beneath the Fallopian tubes—to the left and right of the womb. During childhood the surface of the glands is white and smooth, after puberty it becomes somewhat roughened. The blood supply comes from the uterine and ovarian arteries, the nerve supply from the ovarian and uterine nerves.

Embedded in the ovaries are the *Graafian follicles*—minute hollow spherical bodies. At birth the ovaries of a female infant contain thousands of these tiny, immature follicles—100,000 according to some estimates. They gradually diminish in number up to puberty. At puberty there are only about 10 percent of the original number left. Still these number many thousands —but selection continues until only 400 to 500 mature during the entire lifetime of woman. By the time a woman reaches the menopause, nearly all of the follicles have disappeared—then conception is no longer possible.

Each month a message comes to the ovary selecting one or more ova (eggs) for a journey that can end in conception of a baby or can end in the death of the ovum. Where this message comes from and how it selects just one or several ova is still one of the deep mysteries of life. These several follicles become swollen by the pressure of the fluids within them until at last one breaks through the follicle wall and is expelled. This tiny ovum, which can barely be seen by the naked eyes, is the one selected to be expelled in a gush of fluid. The follicles left behind shrink and regress.

Now the victorious ovum or tiny egg has won the first heat of a race. The second heat starts immediately. The ovum enters the Fallopian tube for a two to three day journey to the womb. It must hurry to keep its rendezvous with the much smaller sperm. If the ovum and sperm meet, the process of fertilization will start. If the ovum does not win the race or if it does not meet any sperm, its life is forfeited. It deteriorates and is lost forever. If the process of fertilization has occurred—the sperm entering the ovum—then pregnancy has begun.

What has happened to the loser of the first heat of the race? This ovum did not die—it only regressed. It has work to do. It must become a temporary endocrine gland. In the Graafian follicle from which the ovum was discharged, the remaining cells start to multiply rapidly until a functional unit is evolved that is known as the *corpus luteum,* the *yellow body,* because of its color. What becomes of this yellow body? If fertilization does not take place between the ovum and sperm, this yellow body develops for about two weeks. Then through a process of absorption, it disappears in about two months, leaving a small scar on the surface of the ovary. If pregnancy does occur the yellow body grows until it is fully developed. It stays fully developed for nearly six months. During the final three months of pregnancy this yellow body gradually recedes.

If reproduction is not begun Nature starts another process. The womb is cleared out—it sheds its lining and secretions. This is the *menstrual period.* This is Nature's way of disposing of the debris of hope. With unsurpassable patience there begins another cycle—the race against time starts all over again. Everything must be made ready for the following month when a new ovum will be released by another follicle. The womb must be prepared for the care and nourishment of a possible embryo. When fertilization finally does occur then menstruation stops!

Do the ovaries secrete some mysterious substance and also give birth to the egg? It is difficult to realize that up to the end of the nineteenth century there were obstetricians who still believed that menstruation was controlled by the nerve fibres in the Fallopian tubes. At that period many gynecologists still thought that all the ovaries supplied was an egg-cell each month.

Doctors Edward Doisy and Edgar Allen of Washington University in St. Louis first demonstrated in 1922 the active female hormones. It was not until 1936 that the hormone estrogen was isolated in pure crystalline form by Doctors MacCorquodale, Thayer, and Doisy who obtained a minute amount of this essence from 4 tons of sows' ovaries. Its structure was soon determined and it was quickly synthesized. This follicular fluid was injected by Doisy and Allen into the body cavity of newly weaned rats. In a few days this injected fluid brought the animals to a state of sexual maturity. These researchers then tried their fluid on older animals, animals without ovaries. Again there were startling reactions. The animals began to show an interest in masculine attention. Their entire genital tract recovered from the atrophy it had undergone after surgery. They were thrown into *estrus* (heat). Estrogen stimulates the growth and maturity of the genital tract, molds the body of the female, causes abundant growth of hair, and is a prime agent in the control of breast and hip development. It also emphasizes, modifies and shapes the traits that charm and fascinate the male.

The ovaries also secrete *progesterone*, which was isolated by Doctors Corner and Allen in 1929. Its chief therapeutic use is in the treatment of threatened natural abortion and irregularities of the menstrual function. A female animal is in heat when she is anxious to be loved. Most women are aware of a greater desire at one phase of their menstrual cycle, shortly before menstruation. This is the time that progesterone levels are highest in her blood.

Estrogen and progesterone provide that balance to a woman for the continuance of the race. Consider what they accomplish. The female genital tract is readied precisely when the ovum matures in its follicle. Then the womb begins to contract with renewed vigor, marking time for the arrival of the sperm. Hardly a cell in the woman's body is unaffected by these physiological preparations for the coming events.

When ovum and sperm meet there is drama, suspense, conflict, complication! When fertilization takes place, the ovum stirs at once to a frenzy of internal activity—every molecule in it becomes intensely excited. The fertilized ovum begins to divide before it even reaches the uterus. It divides and redivides into multiple cells—two, four, sixteen, and ultimately into the many millions of cells that form a human body. For 280 days the embryo lives the life of a parasite. It has attached itself to a living wall from which it derives its sustenance for living and for growth. The nutrients are drawn from the mother. She augments the scant and dwindling food supply with which the egg is charged. The ovum can only grow and develop if it can come in contact with food. These cells remain alive only as long as they are nourished.

Sex glands appear in the embryo by the sixth week of pregnancy. Their future sex, whether male or female, cannot be told at this time—there is no structural difference. Later, under the microscope, cells can be differentiated as male or female—large, rounded cells are female.

Sterility in women may be caused by congenital anatomical defects such as the complete absence of the Fallopian tubes, even though the womb and the ovaries are normal. Then again the womb may be absent or only rudimentary in size even though the ovaries are present and doing their work. In rare instances the vagina may be so small or underdeveloped that normal intercourse is impossible.

Some women become pregnant, then abort or miscarry a few weeks after fertilization. They may do this many times. There are usually two reasons: (1) Anatomically something interfers with the normal development of the fertilized egg so that it is finally expelled from the womb, or (2) there is a failure of the glandular system to support the pregnancy.

For some reasons that are not clearly understood, a woman may menstruate quite regularly but not ovulate. But, if only one of her ovaries is producing eggs, it is still quite possible for a woman to conceive.

7. The Sex Life of Women Over 60

CHANGE OF LIFE, THE *menopause*, usually occurs in women between the ages of forty and fifty-five. This final act of the ovaries is the transition from activity to rest. Menstruation ceases. But sex does not.

The average woman does not reach the peak of her sex drive until she is nearly thirty years old. From then on her sex drive does not decline. Women of middle age are often more capable of full sex gratification than many younger women, maintaining their sex drive until they are in their seventies or eighties.

It is not unusual for women to have a considerable increase in sexual desire just at the menopausal age and afterwards. Realizing she is becoming older, some women have the feeling of wanting to get the most out of life. This may be due to a change in the ovarian output of sex hormones. In this connection, both male and female do have some of the hormones of the opposite sex in their make-up. It is well known that if the male sex hormone is given to a woman it increases the female sex drive.

A classic example of a woman whose sex drive increased to excess after menopause—perhaps because her body contained too much of the male sex hormone—was Catherine the Great of

Russia. Voltaire described her ironically as, "That great man whose name is Catherine!" This energetic Empress had no time for elaborate coquetry. As one biographer wrote, "Her love life resembled that of an important business man!" Born in 1729, a German Princess, Catherine was no beauty. She was a fat, homely Frau—but one who never lacked lovers. There are estimates that they totaled three hundred! In her memoirs she admits to twelve.

Catherine's husband, Peter the Third, was debauched and was regarded by many as an imbecile. After being married ten years, Catherine gave birth to an heir whose paternity was uncertain, because Peter had the reputation of being impotent. Catherine did save the Russian people from her husband, Peter. She succeeded, with the aid of two of her lovers, the Orlov brothers, in securing control of the empire.

Catherine treated many of her lovers as if they were little more than hired prostitutes. She made them officers of the army as long as they pleased her sexually. Most of her lovers were tall, well-built, young and handsome. They were summoned to the palace without warning, received a thorough medical examination, and then to prove their sexual powers were tested for several days by two ladies of the court. Only if he passed these tests was the new lover admitted to Catherine's presence. The Empress also took as lovers older, mature men who gave her advice in matters of state. At the age of sixty-seven, in the arms of her last lover who was over forty years younger, Catherine died of apoplexy!

After the menopause some women refuse sexual intercourse. They feel that sex is only for the young and that after the menopause they are too old. They come to believe that from then on they no longer can please their husbands. They no longer make themselves appealing to their husbands. They neglect their make-up. They pick their clothes for long wearing qualities and not to excite their mate. After the change some—very few—

withdraw completely from the joys of life. They do not realize that resumption of an active sex life will dispel their fears and anxieties.

It may come as a surprise for a great many women that sex and the desire for sex are enjoyable after the menopause—in fact often becoming more satisfying. This desire can build up and up so that women—single, widowed, divorced—seek an outlet, their first choice being a man their own age or a little older. They unashamedly are on the make—they want sex and sometimes marriage. Often marriage after menopause is entirely successful, giving both partners many years of happiness. Not finding a man in their own bracket, some women turn to younger men—they make the advances. There are incidents of older women with sexual relations of this type who give a younger husband a start in life, providing him the financial means for business growth or artistic advancement.

Women after the menopause have a right to association with a younger man. He may appeal in many ways—give her a feeling of being wanted, make her feel young again, and furnish an outlet for her sexual desire. Most often this woman knows that true love is not involved. A more mature man not being available, with time slipping by, she must make a decision—buy favors or do without!

Again referring to the Masters and Johnson report, they found that there is no time limit to the end of sex activity after the menopause. "There seems to be no physiologic reason why the frequency of sexual expression found satisfactory for the younger woman should not be carried over to the postmenopausal years. The frequency of sexual intercourse or manipulative activity during the postmenopausal years is of little import, as long as the individuals concerned are healthy, active, well-adjusted members of society."

Other surveys disclose valuable information on the sex life of women after the menopause. In the fifty to sixty age bracket, nearly all had intercourse and 50 percent indulged more than once a week. At age sixty-five, one half of this group had successful sexual relations.

The change of life period may last from one to three years, sometimes a little longer. During this time menstruation gradually stops (although it has been observed that it can stop suddenly). The ovaries stop maturing eggs and ovulation does not occur. Pregnancy becomes impossible. When menstruation has stopped for a full year a woman can be certain she no longer can conceive. This source of worry for many women is now removed.

After the menopause many women are more excited by sex than ever before. Even a widow who has not enjoyed intercourse for many years will on remarriage again be inflamed, rekindled! This also holds true for a spinster. She will discover that she still has the ability to reach a climax—that her age does not stop her from orgasm. She will discover that her general health is not affected by sex involvement now that she is in her late middle years with the menopause behind her.

After the menopause, there no longer being the fear of pregnancy, the woman can pursue sex with greater concentration, with a display of greater skill for satisfaction. This is often the start of the most enjoyable years in a woman's life—often the most beneficial.

8. The Sex Life of Men Over 60

AFTER MARRIAGE THE YOUNG husband wants his sex after breakfast, after lunch, after dinner, and sometimes in between. He cannot have it often enough to suit his passion. The young wife must go along if he exhausts her in every way—even if her inhibitions are of such magnitude that inwardly she rebels. After about five years of marriage the husband's demands become less and less while the inhibitions that hampered the wife gradually dissolve until she enjoys the act as much as her husband and eagerly looks forward to it.

Midway in life this couple may draw up a sex calendar that will show them the date of their last affair and when they should "bed down" again. As a general rule this does not work out well. When the date rolls around the husband's desire may be at a low ebb while his wife now demands it. The roles of the husband and wife have reversed themselves. His activity and desire can diminish. The wife, now freed from inhibitions and from child-bearing, can become the demanding partner. In the first years of their marriage the excessive needs of the husband were a means for a release from tension—he did not consider his wife, did not know the meaning of sex-love. Later, gaining this knowledge, it is gradually accepted with a good marriage relationship founded on true values.

Excessive sex demands are sometimes made by a husband late in life. With a marriage at sixty or even later, he wants to make up for lost time. When this happens the wife will know how to curb his appetite with just enough sex to keep him potent for many years.

The problem of the man with an insatiable wife calls for a super amount of will power and psychology on his part. Today many women complain, "He doesn't want it often enough;" with the male in this quandary only mentally replying, "She's so demanding—I wish she would let me alone!" In today's complex world, men have become more security troubled, pleasure seems a secondary thing. However, they want to remain potent. According to Masters and Johnson: "The most important factor in the maintenance of effective sexuality for the aging male is consistency of active sexual expression." There should be no anxiety for the male—the sex urge continues into old age. *There is on record an account of a ninety-two year old man engaging in regular sexual relations.*

Reports have been made public by the Institute of Sex Research headed by Alfred C. Kinsey showing the average number of sexual relations at various age levels. Between the ages of twenty-one and twenty-five the average was 3.35 per week. From thirty-one to thirty-five the average dropped to 2.46 per week. From forty-one to forty-five, the average dropped again, to 1.77 per week. Between the ages of fifty-five to sixty, the average dropped below 1 sexual relationship per week—0.89. These are averages. There are tremendous variations. As an instance there was a maximum of 3 acts of intercourse per week in the fifty-five to sixty group.

Studies by Robert L. Dickinson, J. T. Freeman, and others are equally revealing. In a survey of sexual functions in the male with a group of men aged sixty to seventy-four, it was discovered that 55 percent were potent! These men had an average rate of intercouse of nearly 21 per year. In the age group seventy to seventy-five the average frequency of intercourse was 22.8 per year—the average went up with the increase of age in this group revealing that there was no decline of sexual frequency with the advancement of the years. Another study of men sixty-five and older showed that of the large number of men tested, fully 70 percent engaged in sexual intercouse regularly from 1 to 4 times a month. Still another survey of a much older group—men from seventy-five to ninety—showed that nearly 50 percent engaged in coitus with some degree of regularity.

These surveys show that there is a wide variation in the rate of intercourse and potency in all age groups. What is normal for one man is abnormal for another. There can be no hard and fast rule for frequency of sexual intercourse. There are too many physiological and psychological factors involved. The frequency of intercourse is something each couple must work out for themselves.

As the male ages he needs a longer and longer period of rest to recuperate between sex acts. This depends on the man—this is his physiological capacity—it may be an hour, or a day or more. With the wife there can be many acts in a night—this depends on her nervous system. Many wives give themselves so completely, with such intensity, that they are spent and also need a period of recuperation before engaging in the sex act for a second time.

To copulate by a set rule is impossible. The urge must move both partners. It may be twice in a night. It might be once in a week or more. Intelligent people look for the sex activity that will give the greatest fulfillment—the quality act—not the greatest number that they can possibly manage.

Frequency of intercouse can also be affected by lack of privacy, fatigue, a change of habits, changes in work schedules, business tension, or by worry. Eliminating these factors can often increase the frequency of sexual intercourse.

Is there a male change of life—a male climacteric? This is a most controversial concept in the field of medicine. In women there is often no other symptom than the cessation of menstruation to mark her change of life. In the male some physicians deny that a diagnosis can be made while others believe there is enough clinical evidence to defend use of this term.

Some men do experience a change in themselves akin to the menopause in women. The male may experience more or less intense flushes, chills, clammy sweats, and morbid psychic sensations. At the same time nervousness may develop with irritability and fatigue that can lead to melancholia. Energy can be curtailed, and concentration becomes increasingly difficult. Interest in business, social responsibilities, and intellectual pursuits diminish, sometimes disappearing entirely. Life becomes burdensome. He drifts into inactivity. Is this a man's change of life?

For such a man administration of testosterone is helpful—usually bringing outstanding results. Exhaustion and related symptoms vanish. Anxiety gives way to mental calm and to the reawakening of the interests of a normal man.

Another school of thought argues that there is no male menopause—that all the talk on this subject is nonsense. The argument of these experts is that men who have this so-called change remain sexually potent for many years. The subject is certainly debatable. As long as a man can perform satisfactorily, he need not concern himself whether he is going through a change of life!

Impotence in the older man is sometimes caused by the lack of confidence and of stimulation by the female. Long suppression of normal sexual intercourse, especially in a man about his middle fifties, can bring about the tendency to impotence. Normal sexual intercourse with some degree of frequency will often improve this condition.

To the casual observer the usual conception of a "Don Juan" means an irresistible lover and seducer of women—a man whose sexuality is the very opposite of impotence. But psychiatrists now believe that under their appearance of masculine attractiveness, these suave, poised men are really thoroughly neurotic. It is their fear of failure that constantly haunts them, causing sudden impotence early in their lives, generally before they are fifty years old. These men are constantly urged on by insecure fears, frustrations, and anxieties—a need to prove their masculinity! There is no joy or pleasure in the sexual act for these men. The biographies of Don Juan and Casanova support this contention. Every Don Juan discovers at some point in his life that his inferiority emerges and shows up in the form of impotence. There is physical fatigue due to an irregular life, insomnia, a tremendous waste of nervous energy in his constant sexual demands far above the normal.

Often, without being aware of it, the wife can be a contributing factor in the sexual failure of her husband. The more often he fails, the more desirous he is to prove his virility. Here is where a wise wife can assist and help in many ways. There can be increased love play for the man who has difficulty in achieving erection—a gradual arousal to full erection by direct genital touch. By word, attitude and gesture the wife must show that she regards her husband as sexually adequate. Abstaining from sexual relations for a period of time—during which the wife should appear provocative to her husband in the ways she knows by experience will excite him sexually—will help. Promoting his desire and then refusing him for a period of time will bring back his natural aggressiveness and self-confidence. The wife should discover ways to contribute to mutual satisfaction, such as changes in coital position, to discover favorable conditions that will help bring about the desired end.

In healthy individuals extended sexual inactivity can prove disastrous. Nature requires regular activity of the sexual organs. Sexual weakness that is often falsely attributed to the aging process can be caused by inactivity and disuse.

Impotency can be the fault of the male. He makes little or no appeal to his wife's emotions. He goes through the motions.

He does not prepare for the occasion. It's the "same old thing" to him. Finally, the wife shies from the performance. Copulation becomes less frequent, resulting at last in the inability of the male to have an erection.

Some men in their seventies and eighties have difficulty in ejaculating. Sometimes their wives have one or more orgasms before the husband is successful. Administration of testosterone often is effective. Manual stimulation of the genital area by the wife can also contribute to bring about ejaculation. However, this problem is overshadowed by the many men who ejaculate prematurely.

Premature ejaculation can become a habit, a carry-over from many previous years. Both partners are unsatisfied when this occurs. The very anticipation that it will happen can make it happen. To break any habit of long standing is difficult. To break this habit will take time, patience, and training. With an understanding partner there can be success so that normal intercourse will be regained. The female partner can stimulate the male just up to the point of orgasm, then stop completely until the erection dies down. Then she starts all over again, repeating this procedure many times until the male gains control. After some days of this training, intercourse can be attempted and again, when the male feels that he is about to ejaculate, all movement must stop completely—all kissing, all stroking of the body, and all endearing words also must stop. The couple should lie quietly together until the tension subsides; then movement can again be resumed. By this method intercourse that will be mutually fulfilling will be regained.

Premature ejaculation is probably one of the main causes of unsuccessful marriage. It is prevalent in the young man. It is widespread among the mature man. Sometimes it is caused by an overly sensitive male sexual mechanism. The head of the penis may be so sensitive that the male has no control. Ejaculation occurs when he touches the female genitals. In addition to the physical aspect there may be an emotional one wherein the

the male may be intensely passionate and unable to control the excitement of intercourse. These problems also can be overcome by training with the aid of a considerate partner.

For men past middle life the term *prostate* is something that often arouses needless fear. Although there is no evidence that the prostate has any influence on sexual traits it is an important accessory sexual organ. If the prostate is removed, sexual desire and potency are unaffected—the prostate is not essential. Its principal function is to contribute a thin fluid, a constituent of semen, as a transport medium for spermatozoa. As a muscle it contracts at ejaculation forcing the semen into the urethra and then out of the penis. As the prostate sits like a collar around the neck of the bladder, enlargement can make it difficult to urinate. Should an operation be necessary, it is not true that it will make the man impotent. He can with certain types of surgical procedure function sexually as well as before the operation; however, the ejaculation will back into his bladder. Impregnating a woman with sperm will then be impossible.

A prostate operation is not always necessary. Enlargement can be treated medically by the use of drugs. Prostate massage is also a therapy measure. Sexual function depends on the male —if sexually active before surgery he will remain so afterwards. It must be reiterated—*prostate surgery does not end a man's sexual activity!*

9. When Men Over 60 Marry

ANCIENT RECORDS SHOW THAT for thousands of years older men have sought to prove and enhance their virility by marrying girls much younger than themselves. In ancient Egypt girls were married from the ages of twelve to fourteen with the supposition that these virtuous girls restored the sexual powers of their much older husbands. Moslems place great faith in young women as rejuvenating forces. The prophet Mohammed gave them a tradition that young girls can succor old men—at an advanced age Mohammed took two wives, one was seven and the other was eight! To this day slavers in the Middle East supply young girls to rich old men—the purpose is not for wild sex orgies, but to provide benefits to the tired old bones as the young girls "radiate" their youth. The English friar Roger Bacon, most discreetly as behooves a monk, advanced the same method for reviving wizened older members of the nobility.

In our own times selection of a mate by a man over sixty is often associated with his attitude about children. Does he want children—does he want to perpetuate his name? If the answer is yes, he must marry a woman who can give him an issue—a younger woman who has not reached her menopause. This might mean a great age difference between husband and wife. Should he impregnate his wife when he is age sixty or over? If so, when he reaches eighty his child will be twenty. This type of man, and there are many, does ponder this problem. Often his desire is overwhelmingly powerful to protect and perpetuate his name.

There are also women who passionately believe that they must perpetuate the race—they must give the world children. This desire often takes precedence over self-preservation—the first law of nature. These women feel childbirth is their duty—the sole reason they are on this earth. If this desire is unfulfilled their life seems incomplete.

An age difference of five years in marriage is considered average—the male five years older than his wife. When the male is ten years older this seems to be considered a large difference. When the man of sixty contemplates marrying a woman of about thirty-five, the spread is indeed great.

Older men marrying younger women are usually youthful in many ways. They enjoy young social relationships. They think young and are physically virile. The young woman contemplating this kind of marriage usually does not do so for some such neurotic reason as wanting a father-type husband. The younger woman marrying the older man usually is expressing her maturity—she prefers older men to those of her own age.

A man of sixty should find adjustment to married life not too difficult. He has had sexual relationships. He is not marrying a woman of sixty who has never had sexual experience but a young woman who looks forward to a satisfying sex life. For her the transition also will not be difficult.

How can any man know if the new relationship is truly one of love? He must know if she is healthy and if she can bear the children he desires. For the young woman, the mental competence of her older mate is of utmost importance—she must know if her contemplated husband is fully aware of the marriage responsibilities. The answers to some of these questions can be found before marriage—some can only be answered after the ceremony.

The mature male with thoughts of children will not rush into a marriage. He will select a woman who is intellectually his equal, because he wants his children to be bright and alert and to become a success in the world.

This avails him nothing if he cannot impregnate his wife with live sperm that will fertilize her ova. A first requisite is a test of his sperm—a sperm count—to discover if there are live sperm and if there are sufficient in his ejaculation so that there is a possibility of impregnation. Should this report show negative results and the wife be completely healthy there is still a method of producing a child—artificial insemination.

Thousands of "test tube" babies have been born in the United States. When the husband produces sperm, artificial insemination is used if he cannot deposit semen in the vagina or when vaginal discharges prevent the sperm from traveling to the egg. A donor may supply sperm to be deposited into the wife. The donor is usually a medical student. His identity is kept secret. The physician tries to select a donor about the same size as the husband with similar eye, hair, and skin coloring. As the donor is thoroughly investigated, his traits will be beyond reproach and his intelligence of a high degree.

The physician will deposit the semen either in the vagina or directly in the mouth of the womb. Sometimes semen from the husband will be mixed with that of the donor, creating the possibility that the husband will be the actual father of the child. Often the physician will urge the couple to have intercourse after the injection, which again places doubt on the real paternity of the child.

It is generally agreed that the size of the penis, whether large or small, is unimportant in achieving conception. The fully erect smaller penis can and does function as a dilating agent as effectively as a larger penis.

In intercouse it is the man who supplies the ejaculation. The physical exertion and the psychic tension are about equal for male and female. There is no great demand made on the male if there has been time for the sperm to accumulate in sufficient quantity. Trying to follow a first coitus with a second in too short a time can mean an enormous strain on the sensitive local nerves and tissues of the various organs that supply and store the semen. Many men, whether in their twenties or sixties or over, cannot meet this demand. There must be time for replenishment. Some men take only an hour or two, some men might need a day or two.

Professor Metchnikoff in his *Etudes Sur la Nature Humaine* states that he has seen many men between ninety-four and one hundred-and-four years of age who have suffered from copious seminal emissions. Upon examination of these emissions he found large numbers of live normal spermatozoa. These men at an advanced age had life-giving properties. Why is nature so prodigal of sperm, so wasteful, since only one of countless millions can fertilize an egg-cell and awaken new life? The answer is not known!

Birth control problems arise when a potent older man is married to a woman who can bear a child or perhaps several children. This couple may decide that their family is large enough, that the husband wants to be a father to his children and not appear to them as a grandfather—a child of fifteen with a father seventy-five! Or there might be many other reasons why some form of birth control is desired. These reasons can be economic, social, or psychological. Mental and physical considerations are another possibility.

Some people have an aversion to the birth control pill; there are some who dislike condoms, coitus interruptus, the diaphragm, jellies, creams, tablets, rings, or suppositories!

Castration will make the husband sterile—often destroying the sex drive. Few physicians will perform such an operation unless there is some great and urgent need.

For the wife there can be sterilization, a hospital procedure, where the Fallopian tubes are cut and tied off. This prevents any meeting of sperm and ova, making conception impossible.

A method of birth control that has appealed to thousands of couples is male sterilization, or *vasectomy*. This procedure can be performed in the physician's office. Cutting and tying the sperm tubes prevents sperm, which are produced in the testicles, from traveling through the sperm tubes. This shuts off the pathway of sperm so that they cannot be ejaculated, and it leaves the testicles to function in an otherwise normal manner. The physician always explains to his patient that this is a permanent condition—it cannot be reversed by another simple operation at some future date. Vasectomy is final and irreversible. After a few weeks a semen specimen is checked to see if the operation is successful. If the result is negative no further check is necessary—the husband cannot fertilze the ova.

Vasectomy will not make a man impotent. It will not change his ability to have an erection. It will not stop him from ejaculating. It only prevents the semen from containing sperm. With valid reasons for a vasectomy there should be no emotional conflicts. It should result only in peace of mind, with perhaps an improvement in marital relations, if the fear of pregnancy has been an impediment of harmony between husband and wife.

After vasectomy some husbands and wives find their sexual drive more demanding, leading to more frequent intercourse. Many couples claim their enjoyment of sex is greater. Some men boast that they now can bring their wives more quickly to a climax. But vasectomy makes some men feel sexually incomplete, sexually inadequate. The operation itself does not hinder the husband's ability to engage in intercourse, providing he was and is potent.

10. Can You Turn Back the Hands of Time?

CAN THE VIGOR AND virility of youth be regained? This perennial question has been the subject of countless books, articles, experiments, investigations, adventures, speculations, and endeavors. The ancient Greeks and Romans sought potions and amulets, and Spanish conquistador Ponce de Leon explored Florida seeking the elusive "Fountain of Youth." But it was not until the late 1800's that scientists began making real headway in the eternal quest.

On the evening of June 1, 1889, Charles Edouard Brown-Sequard stood before the members of the Societe de Biologie. They had gathered to hear news of an important discovery. The members smiled warmly at their friend and comrade. In his lectures there were always words of scientific wisdom. They waited expectantly. The seventy-two-year-old Brown-Sequard had helped organize this society. He was the esteemed Professor of Physiology at the University of Paris. He held a place of honor in the world of science.

Then Brown-Sequard read his report. He told the members how his strength had gradually diminished during the past ten or twelve years—how a few weeks previously he became too weak to work continuously and how he had been too exhausted by his work even to sleep. Then, after many experiments and aflame with hope, he plunged a hypodermic needle into his own body. During the past three weeks he had injected himself ten times—first using testicular material obtained from young dogs that were in their prime of life, and then switching to extracts from young guinea pigs.

Professor Brown-Sequard stood straight before his audience —seeming much younger than his seventy-two years. He said that a few days after the first subcutaneous injection there began a radical change that accelerated as the injections were added one after the other. Now, he told the members, he had regained the strength of many years ago; his laboratory work was again a pleasure; he could work hour after·hour; he again took a stroll after his dinner; and he easily walked up and down stairs where formerly he needed assistance. He told his audience how he had tested himself in many ways, such as the weights he now could lift. He claimed he was a new man—that he had been rejuvenated.

He waited for the acclaim and applause. But this audience of scientists was skeptical. Instead of cheers and bravos, there was a thunder of jeers and boos! Brown-Sequard was all but hooted out of the hall!

The newspapers of Paris were filled the next day with reports of Brown-Sequard's 'rejuvenation.' He was beset by an army of older men, all eager and anxious to try this new elixir for a resumption of the rite of Venus.

But the scientific press and the medical press were flooded with articles and editorials filled with sarcasm and attacks on Brown-Sequard. All the remarkable scientific work of a lifetime of service to mankind was forgotten.

Before he died in 1894, Brown-Sequard admitted that perhaps he was mistaken about the physical rejuvenation attributed to injections—that perhaps he received psychological benefits from his glowing faith in the extracts. Brown-Sequard did not know how close he was to an important discovery. He did not know he was using the wrong solvent or that the male hormones are not stored in the testicles. Scientist though he was, when it came to an experiment on himself, he could not differentiate between subjective and objective results—the changes a patient thinks he feels and the changes that can be measured by test and physical observation.

Nevertheless, Brown-Sequard did crash through the so-called 'law' of nature. His was the earliest scientific approach to the possibility of rehabilition through chemical treatment. He made possible much of the creative work that followed. Today his basic theories are universally conceded. He did not discover the 'Elixir of Youth' or 'The Pillar of Fire' or a magic fountain or spring. He showed that chemical substances secreted by the endocrine glands influence the activity of other glands—that all are responsible for spectacular effects on personality, the sex drive, vitality, and virility!

It is just a short leap in time from Brown-Sequard to Doctor Serge Voronoff who announced his discovery on October 18, 1919, before the members of the 28th French Surgical Congress. At this time he described the rejuvenation of a goat that was so far advanced in senility that it had lost its hair and could hardly stand. After treatment this animal was transformed. Not only did it regain health and vigor, but it was mated successfully with a young female, becoming in the course of time the parent of a healthy kid. The announcement of the experiment raised a great furor.

Doctor Voronoff gave the members of the Congress details of his rejuvenation technique. He had transplanted the sex glands of a vigorous young male goat into the senile animal. After his announcement he was besieged by hordes of men who wanted to regain their sexual vigor. Among these men were many not extremely old, but who for one reason or another could not give sexual satisfaction to their bedfellows.

Voronoff, the scientist, dreamed of testing out his method on a human being. He had plenty of men who would submit willingly to the operation and in addition pay a fee for the privilege. His problem was to find glands suited to transplantation into the human body. Now and again, the glands of men who had lost their lives by accident were available. Here again there were serious problems—the glands must come from young human testicles, they must be transplanted while still fresh, and there was always the possibility that the victim might have been diseased. There was no time to thoroughly examine the donor—there could not be any delay if success was to be achieved. Voronoff even considered buying a testicle—just one—from some young man, and then decided against this plan. He tried to secure the testicles from a man who passed away from natural causes, only to become involved in tremendous opposition from the authorities and from the clergy. In this dilemma his reasoning led him to animals. He decided to work with the monkey. After experimentation he became convinced that monkey glands were as potent as the human gland.

In 1920, ten years after he began his series of experiments, Voronoff removed the testis of a twelve year old chimpanzee and transplanted it into the body of a seventy-four-year-old man. The operation consisted in removal of the male testis from the monkey and separating this testicle into segments. Doctor Voronoff then opened the scrotum of his patient and applied the segments to the scarified surface of the tunica vaginalis—the membrane that covers the testicle and is its supply source of blood. Finally, the scrotum was closed.

The result of the experiment was fantastic. Voronoff reported that his patient had gained a new lease on life—his appetite improved, his strength returned, his vigor revived, his hair started to grow again, and his skin became firm and smooth. Whatever new difficulties might appear, the first round of the battle had been won.

Voronoff publicized his results. Men from all over the world offered fortunes for the "monkey gland" operation. After a few years Voronoff had a sheaf of testimonials—some from men who were still rejuvenated after one year, and some from men who had had the operation three years previously. Voronoff saw his supply of captive apes dwindle. He dreamed of a monkey farm—he saw far into the future when there would be depositories of testicles, ovaries, and perhaps other spare parts for the body.

So great was the pressure on Voronoff that he decided to breed his own African chimpanzees. He moved his headquarters to the Chateau Grimaldi at Ventimeglia, between France and Italy. Soon, in this haven, he had several hundred monkeys ready to provide fresh, healthy gland tissue as the need arose.

Voronoff did not forget the females. In a publication, he wrote: "Transplantation has previously been a practice confined almost exclusively to men. Our newer research shows that it can be applied with equal effectiveness to women. Work in this field was started several years ago and our success has been considerable. In practice, there is hardly more difficulty in rejuvenation of women than of men. Transplantation is accomplished with use of a local anesthetic, because no organ is removed—one is added. Effects of the operation begin to show themselves after a few months. Generally it takes about a full year before the effects are evident. When I see my patients after that period, I can hardly recognize them. Their eyes glitter, their movements are lively and elastic. They appear to be young women. They seem younger mentally—their power of thinking is strengthened, their activity unbelievable. Children born to parents, one of whom has undergone a transplantation are remarkably healthy, and possess all the potentialities for becoming outstanding human beings. A physician friend of mine once showed me a photograph of the three-year old son of one of his patients. 'His father,' he said, 'is seventy. Immediately after a rejuvenation operation he fell in love with my secretary and married her.'"

Despite the enthusiastic accounts of Doctor Voronoff, transplantation remained uncertain in effect, and expensive beyond the means of most persons. Moreover, the striking benefits of the operation wore off in two or three years.

There are many difficulties in making a successful gland transplantation. The best hope of success in this field lies in the substitution of glands between the same species. When goat or monkey glands are transplanted into human begins the life expectancy of the gland is relatively short. Unable to survive in an environment chemically hostile, the transplanted gland may seem to thrive for a time, and then gradually it loses vitality.

Even gland transplants between members of the same species, man-to-man for instance, are of uncertain duration. Even grafts from close relations will not "take," as witness skin grafts which must come from the person himself or herself. Father, mother, sister, or brother cannot supply the necessary material. The only exception is an identical twin. There can be a connection between the transplanted tissue and the blood supply for a time, and then comes a reaction. The body usually will not accept permanently the tissue of another person.

Doctor Voronoff's work was of incalculable value, but his procedure came to a dead end. The "monkey-gland man" faded into oblivion. But, latching onto the Voronoff fad, here in America another man started a sex rejuvenation operation—this time with a more plentiful animal, the goat! He was the late Doctor John Brinkley. Starting his campaign—for it must be called just that—in Kansas, his business immediately boomed. He broadcast his message from his own powerful radio station. Brinkley became a household word as his operations were publicized far and wide. His customers came from all parts of the country. Soon he came into conflict with the authorities. Brinkley was forced to move to Mexico. Again he used a powerful radio station to beam his goat gland message. Soon the goat gland technique and business collapsed—the method was a total failure.

Eugen Steinach, an Austrian physician, was another great name in the field of rejuvenation. In 1910 Steinach organized the first laboratory in Germany for general and comparative psysiology. There he worked on many sex experiments. Beginning with transplantation of rat testes, he proved conclusively that man's secondary sex forms and sex traits depend entirely on secretions from the interstitial cells of the testes. In 1912, Steinach went a step further. He castrated infant male guinea pigs, and then planted ovaries in the resulting neuters. In the developing animals, milk-producing nipples appeared, body and hair growth approached nearer to the feminine pattern than to the masculine. These feminized animals seemed to arouse quite as much ardor in normal males as though born with ovaries. Still more striking was the mother instinct they displayed. Normal males are without paternal instinct, driving away young ones of their kind; but these feminized males actually suckled the young. Infant female guinea pigs were spayed, and then supplied with testes. They then uttered guttural masculine sounds insead of feminine squeaks and pursued normal females that were in heat.

Steinach experimented with rats at different temperatures. He and a zoologist found that in a hot climate the rats' interstitial cells developed to a greater degree than in a cool climate, with resulting enlargement of secondary sex characteristics and much more sexual excitability. This probably accounts for the greater sexuality of tropical and semi-tropical men as compared with men in temperate zones.

Another brilliant idea entered the fertile mind of this doctor. Instead of introducing a foreign substance into the body, that is the testes, why not use the person's own secretions? He proposed a simple procedure—simply tie up the duct bearing away the products of the testes—tie up the vas deferens, the sperm tube! He reasoned that the pressure of the dammed up seminal fluids would cause the delicate sperm-producing tissues to atrophy and then they would be replaced by the sturdier interstitial cells. This reasoning was supported by experimental work on animals.

There always comes a time when an experiment must be tried on a human. Steinach was anxious to prove his theory. The first subject was a coachman, who at age forty-three could hardly walk, and weighed only 108 pounds—a sickly, unhappy man. Steinach persuaded a surgeon to perform a vasoligation operation on this poor human. Soon a suture tied off the flow of sperm forever.

Steinach claimed the result was a miracle—that the coachman was completely rejuvenated, that he was charged with great vitality. Now came operation after operation—on a man of sixty-seven, on a man in his eighties, on men of all ages. All the reports were glorious successes. After the operations the patients became energetic and cheerful; their endurance was remarkable; and their appetite was enormous. Steinach even claimed that his patients lost any illnesses they had and that their eyesight improved—in short there was a regeneration of the entire organism.

It is believed that thousands of men went through the operation at that time. It is a relatively simple office procedure performed under local anesthesia. Ligating the vas prevents the ejaculation of sperm though it does not interfere otherwise with the sex act. But Steinach's theory that a resurgence of vigor would come from an increase of the hormone-secreting cells of the testis at the expense of the sperm producing cells seems to be ill-founded. After a few months the patient usually is no better off than before the operation. Large amounts of male hormone being forced into the blood stream by pressure of the dammed-up seminal fluid may give temporary vigor. Men who seek vasoligation for renewed vigor generally have an inadequate day-to-day supply of male hormone from their own factory. Today it is accepted as a birth-control measure, but then it was described as a rejuvenate.

Steinach's ligation is not applicable to women because of the different anatomical construction of the ovaries. In his later years this problem occupied him. He wanted to do something for the female. The transplantation of ovaries was seldom successful. His search centered upon a hormone extract able to initiate the sexual cycle and to reactivate the female organism. This time he started to work with cattle—an effort to combat sterility among the herds in Switzerland. The high cost of treatment and the necessary training of the operators prevented his method from becoming of practical value, although he claimed great success in this work.

Up to the time of his death in 1944 at age eighty-four, Steinach retained his vitality—he was his own guinea pig. Like so many pioneers, today he is all but forgotten by the public and by the scientific fraternity.

The Prolongation of Life was written by Nobel prize winner Elie Metchnikoff when he was just over sixty years of age. He had taught zoology at Odessa, and later traveled to Sicily where he formulated the doctrine of *phagocytosis*, the destruction of bacteria by the white blood corpuscles. Caring nothing for either position or fortune, this true scientist gave up his post in 1888 to work under Pasteur in Paris. He received the Nobel prize in 1908.

When Metchnikoff devoted his thought to sex and age, he connected it with his phagocyte theory. Phagocytes destroy bacteria, and also annihilate the cellular debris. At birth the store of nerve cells is fixed for the entire life span—nerve cells cannot be renewed. Slowly, as life continues year after year, there is a steady loss in the quantity of these nerve cells. Metchnikoff believed that the nerve cells become weakened by cellular debris and are destroyed by the neuronophages—the devourers of nerve cells.

For a long time Metchnikoff tried to discover the cause of this degeneration. He attributed it to the poisoning of the organism. He came to the conclusion that it is caused by the presence of putrescent toxins in the large intestine. In studies of the comparative lengths of the large intestine in different species of animals, he was impressed by its absence in certain types. After much research he concluded that the large intestine was not only useless but actually harmful to the human organism!

He believed there could be only one solution to this problem. The putrefactive bacteria must be engulfed by an acid so that they could not grow. He remembered that Bulgarian peasants lived to ripe old ages and that they drank yogurt. The lactic acid-producing organism, *Lactobacillus Bulgaricus*, was a prime constituent of this milk drink. Metchnikoff gave his secret to the world which promptly went on a yogurt binge. Everyone wanted to live as long as the Bulgarians—everyone wanted strength and vigor for sexual gratification. Today, as a sex stimulant yogurt is forgotten, although as a source of food it is consumed in huge quantities.

The work of Metchnikoff was carried on in a strange direction by his pupil, Professor Alexander Alexandrovitch Bogomolets. He was the director of the Institute of Experimental Biology and Pathology of the Ukraine, later President of the Academy of Science of the Ukraine in Kiev. He also began to ponder the problem of prolonging sex life and prolonging life itself.

Bogomolets decided to reverse the findings of Metchnikoff, by proving that the real danger to life did not lie in activity of the phagocytes but in the tendency of the entire system to generate fiber! This was an original thought, but it also presented many problems.

He described old age as "the loss of the power of regeneration." By this statement he directly connected the problem with the greater or lesser capacity of the cells to re-create themselves. He invented the ACS serum that he claimed would become a factor of stimulation and regeneration of the connective tissue and through it the tissues and cells of the entire body. This was encouraging news. Many meanings were read into his remarks that were not there—that his serum cured arthritis, cancer, and split personality. Bogomolets, however, made no such claims. This cautious scientist saw no reason why men should not learn to live to the age of 150. He wrote, "A man of sixty or seventy is still young. He has lived only half of his natural life." Bogomolets named many factors that are involved in ageing—food, vitamins, exercise, environment, body chemistry, electrical force, sexual frequency, and hormones. But the battle, he wrote, must begin with the mother even before the new life is conceived and must continue all through the months in the womb and the years in the outside world. But Bogomolets and his serum, like Metchnikoff and his therapy, soon faded from the scene. He became enamored of his product, and became the victim of wishful thinking in which he twisted biology to his own purpose.

Man's fond hopes are always aroused by some system or technique. As soon as one fades away another is publicized in the press. Only a few years ago it was the "novocain theory" developed by Doctor Anna Aslan in Roumania. Why novocain might be thought a rejuvenant is a mystery. For years it has been used to block nerves as a spinal anethesia. Here again publicity sent many men rushing to their physicians for a novocain injection! Investigators from this country noted that Doctor Aslan's novocain therapy was officially accepted as legitimate in the Soviet Union. Physicians in this country report that their results were not encouraging when tested under clinical controls.

Professor Paul Niehans in Switzerland developed injections of cells from unborn lambs to rejuvenate men. This technique is still in practice in various parts of Europe and in this country. That Doctor Niehans treated several world famous men is established by documentation—that they received added years of sexual enjoyment combined with splendid health is still under investigation.

Scientists today are elaborating a new theory. Stop the ageing process when a person is fully mature so that he or she will remain mature for a long time. With chickens as their testing animal, it was discovered that an acid called *tryptophan* causes growth and ageing. This acid is one of the chemicals present in protein and is essential to growth. It activates the pituitary gland and is helpful in producing secretions that are needed for normal growth. Extracting all of the trypotophan acid from the foods fed to the experimental chickens immediately stopped the ageing process.

Can this be applied to man? Man awaits the answer!

11. The Role of Endocrine Glands in Sex

OVER THE YEARS it had been observed from time to time that when certain small glands were removed from the body, marked chemical and structural changes take place. Scientists came to the conclusion that these glands furnished some secretion to the blood that influenced the chemical processes of the body. It was discovered that there were glands of external secretion, such as the salivary, sweat, tear, and other glands that have a duct—a tube through which the secretion flows to the exterior of the body or into another body, such as the liver that secretes bile. And it was discovered that there also were glands of internal secretion —glands that form within their cells specific chemical substances called *hormones* that pass directly into the blood stream. Some glands produce a double secretion, one internal that is taken up by the blood stream and one external that is excreted by way of a duct. For example, the male sex glands have this double feature.

Where did the word *hormone* come from? Two English physiologists named these internal secretions hormones from the Greek verb for *rouse* or *set in motion*. The hormones are like little telegraph boys sent from one part of the body to another to "excite," to "rouse." Their presence increases activity in the cells they visit.

Medical science through many years has pinpointed the action of these glands. Each *endocrine gland* (gland of internal secretion) manufactures one or more specific hormones that affects certain cells, tissues, or entire organs. They work in unison, cooperating with one another, exerting a positive influence on each other and on the tissue with which they come in contact. The endocrine glands and their hormones can equip you for a life of effective happiness. They may make you too tall or too short, too fat or too lean, too tense or too relaxed, or too alert or too dull. They may endow you with a warm passion or cast you in a mold of sexual frigidity. They may retard the growth of your mind or accelerate the tempo of learning, supplying you with a ready intelligence and wisdom. In all things that contribute to the joy of living the hormones can enrich with great gifts. The manifestations of their phenomena gives a clear conception how marvelously the human organism operates, how it thrives, and how it keeps alive!

The Pituitary—the Master Gland

A biographer of Napoleon describes him at age fifty—"the Emperor's virility was exhausted; he had lost all interest in sex; he had already begun to suffer from disappearance of hair on his body, atrophy of the genital organs and an extreme fineness of the skin. The result was total sexual frigidity." He was only fifty-two years of age when he died, fat and unable to think clearly—due to pituitary gland insufficiency! This is the opinion of many experts!

This provides food for thought. A gland that can so change a man must be large and heavy. Is it? No— the pituitary is only about as big as the tip of the little finger. It is not heavy, about one gram, one fifth as much as a five-cent piece. It is larger in women than in men!

Place a finger-tip in one ear canal pointing straight through the head to the opposite ear. The pituitary hangs from the base of the brain, approximately at the middle point of the imaginary line from ear to ear. It is fantastic that such a tiny organ has the power to control human lives.

Being of such great importance, Nature has housed this gland in a pocket of sphenoid bone called the *Turk's saddle*. Here reigns this hidden dictator, exerting chemical control on countless ways of living. Nature also protected the gland in another way. It is surrounded on all sides by the most remarkable circular blood stream in the entire body, so that it is almost impossible to deprive it of blood.

When working in harmony with the other endocrine glands, the pituitary gland insures keen mental powers well into old age, favors a skeleton that is strong and firm, regulates the nerves so that they are steady, and sees that the sensory faculties remain acute to a ripe old age.

How is this known? By laborious experiment on animals followed by tests on humans. It has been proven that the pituitary gland, small as it is, controls practically all the other glands. It controls growth, development, sexual maturity, blood pressure, pregnancy, menstruation, the water exchange of the body, and many of the biochemical ingredients of the blood!

Until recently, the sex glands or gonads, were regarded as the sole source and regulators of sex characteristics. But now it has been established that the pituitary exerts an almost autocratic control over the sex glands themselves. This means that any disturbance of the pituitary is bound to affect the gonads, resulting in deficient development of the genitals, frigidity, faulty menstruation, and—in the male—lack of virility!

Doctors Philip Smith and Earl Engle of Stanford University proved beyond doubt that the pituitary gland controls sex maturity. If this gland is in place and functioning, laboratory animals mature sexually in normal time. With the gland removed, sex maturity is delayed or prevented completely. But even if the gland is removed, sexual maturity can still be produced by injecting the animal with an extract of pituitary substance. Pituitary injections have been tried on impotent men over sixty with good results. Work by several physicians in this field continues. Many of their patients return to a life of regular sexual intercourse.

A defective pituitary can cause a small penis or sexual impotence. As the master gland, it stimulates other glands, including the sex glands, into action. But ageing itself is not the result of pituitary failure. There is no evidence available that suggests pituitary injections will slow the ageing process.

The pituitary is the conductor of the orchestra of endocrine glands—with the brain presiding over the pituitary to which it is attached. The awakening of the sex glands that bring childhood to an end and start adolescence and the control of growth that insures the attainment of full adult size make the pituitary the biological timekeeper.

The Pineal—Gland of Mystery

There is another endocrine gland in the head—the *pineal*. In proportion to its size, perhaps no body structure is more interesting. It is a solid reddish-grey organ 8 mm. in length and 5 mm. in width, shaped much like a pine cone. It is suspended by a stalk just behind the mid-brain, behind and above the pituitary.

This tiny gland has been a mystery that has intrigued scientists for hundreds of years. The theory has been advanced that there is a physiological tie-up between the pineal and the sex development involving children from two to sixteen years of age. Study of many cases suggest that the pineal is in some way related to sexual maturity. Young rats injected with pineal extract remain undersized in stature but show a genital over-development and over-activity. The full effects of the extract appear only in later generations, and if these generations receive similar treatment they produce in turn still more sexually precocious offspring. That the pineal acts as a regulator for the sex hormone of the pituitary gland, as a protection from premature sexual development, seems a possibility.

The Thyroid—Life's Pace Maker

The background of knowledge about the thyroid gland dates back as far as 2000 B.C. Hindu doctors referred to the swelling of the thyroid as *goiter*. Egyptian surgeons removed thyroid goiters. The Romans thought such swellings were caused by impure water. In 1180 A.D., Roger of Palermo used ground sponge and seaweed in his efforts to cure goiter. Because the iodine content of both is high, he undoubtedly achieved success in many of his patients. Why his discovery was not followed through remains a mystery. However, it was not until the beginning of the nineteenth century that the clinical importance of this gland was fully appreciated.

There are certain regions in the world in which there is a marked lack of iodine. Here, it is recognized that the absence of iodine is responsible for thyroid enlargement. Switzerland, France, Germany, Canada, and our own country all present well-marked goiter districts in which there are many people suffering from various degrees of the disorder.

There are definite goiter districts in Oregon, Montana, and Nevada. In the Salt Lake valley, on the other hand, the proximity to salt water makes goiter a relatively uncommon condition. It is significant that in goiter districts that there is a definite lack of iodine in the water and in the soil. Widespread cases of goiter are almost unknown in seaboard areas. Japan, for example, has comparatively few cases. The Japanese make seaweed a staple in their diet. Wherever seafood is eaten plentifully, goiter is rare.

Now that it has been recognized that lack of iodine is partly responsible for thyroid enlargement, iodine is added to the water reservoirs of many towns and cities. As a result goiter is fast disappearing as an endemic disease in this country.

The thyroid gland is located in the front part of the neck,

astride the Adam's apple. It is composed of two oval-shaped lobes, one on each side of the neck and connected at their lower ends by a small crossbar known as the *isthmus*. The entire gland weighs about one ounce and varies from two to three inches in width. It is larger in women than in men. During adolescence, menstruation, pregnancy, and menopause it becomes still larger. What unbelievable power is packed into this small amount of tissue—power to make or break a human life!

The thyroid occupies the important position of driver at the controls, in complete charge of the gear shift and accelerator mechanisms of the physiologic functions. It determines the speed of life. The thyroid increases sensitivity to normal stimuli, mental and physical. It governs to an extraordinary degree the ever-changing flow of the emotions. It serves as an emotional shock absorber, guarding against mental trauma. It accelerates the assimilation of fats, regulates the growth of bones and teeth, and controls the texture and quality of the skin. It is physiologically linked with all the other glands in the body and has a supporting influence on these glands.

Does the thyroid effect the sex glands? There is a close and sympathetic relationship between the thyroid and the sex glands of men and women. This can be explained by the fact that sexual function is, after all, an expression of energy; and, since the thyroid is the governor of the uses of energy, there is a close association.

Famous French physicist, Henri Becquerel carried a small vial of radium in his vest pocket when he went to London to give a lecture. This was in 1901. A few weeks later he noticed a reaction on the skin of his abdomen. This led him to the thought—if radium rays could injure healthy tissue they might be used to destroy diseased tissue. This led by a series of steps in 1941 to the administration of radioactive iodine.

It is a curious fact that too much calcium in the diet predisposes the individual to goiter even though his iodine intake is adequate. Dairy regions are sometimes goiter centers. Also there appears to be a substance in cabbage which, when consumed in large quantities, increases the thyroid's need for iodine. In areas where cabbage abounds, goiter is likely to be extensive.

The Parathyroids—the Lime Reservoirs

The smallest of the endocrine glands of the body are the *parathyroids*. Oval in shape, yellowish red to brownish red in color, they are imbedded in the thyroid tissue like grains of wheat. No wonder they escaped detection for so many years. Each is about the size of the head of an ordinary pin.

The parathyroids are situated on both sides of the thyroid. In quantity there have been found as many as twelve and as few as one—the normal amount being four. These four weigh less than a gram. Because of their shape and appearance they were first thought to be lymph nodes.

Some years ago it was commonly believed that eating meat produced tetany (spasm) after the removal of the thyroid. Vegetarianism received a tremendous boost in consequence. Inquiring minds wanted to see if this was a scientific fact. Scientists removed the thyroid glands of plant-eating animals. These animals did not have the dreaded convulsions after this operation. In consequence, eating vegetables became more than a fad—it seemed certain that eating meat was the cause of the terrible spasms. However, this theory was exploded when a veterinarian discovered that in animals the thyroid was distant from the parathyroids. The operation on the animals did not remove the parathyroids—the eating of meat was resumed with relish!

The principal function of the parathyroids is to regulate the calcium supply of the body. Up to the present no association has been made between these tiny glands and the ageing process, nor has their role in sex life been defined. However, they are apparently vital to proper nutrition, bone development, general growth, and life.

There are no parathyroids in fish. Why? The sea, as an all-surrounding and all providing source of salts, makes it unnecessary.

The Thymus—Gland of Immunity

Imagine a pigeon looking at the eggs she has just laid and then flying away from her nest. The eggs could not be hatched—they were without shells. Surely an embarrassing moment for any pigeon. What caused the pigeon to lay these peculiar eggs? By surgery her thymus gland had been removed. Could she ever again lay eggs with shells, eggs that could be hatched? Yes—by feeding her dried thymus!

At present there is no certainty that this organ is really an endocrine gland. It is located in the chest not far below the thyroid gland. By placing the thumb and forefinger on opposite sides of the collarbone, the bone that spreads just below the throat, the flat of the hand will cover the area of the thymus.

The thymus has a rich blood supply. At birth this gland is pinkish in color. Later in life it becomes gray. Still later it turns yellowish as the blood supply decreases. The thymus also changes in weight. At birth it weights from a fourth to half an ounce. At puberty its weight increases to more than an ounce. Then it begins to shrink and diminish in activity until by the age of fifty the gland is back to its original birth weight and has become connective tissue, lymphatic tissue, and fat.

Thyme, the fragrant herb, has been used for centuries in medicine and as a flavoring in cooking. Because the gland looks like a cluster of thyme, Galen named this gland the thymus. The herb thyme is used to flavor soups or roast; the gland thymus is served on the dinner table as sweetbreads. In humans the thymus does fulfill a most important physiologic role—inhibiting the growth and activity of the sex glands during childhood.

If the activity of the thymus persists beyond childhood into adolescence, the sex gland and the sex traits fail to mature—a fine featured angelic look results along with transparent skin, silken hair, a delicately moulded body, and quick and graceful movement.

That the thymus plays an important role in the body is shown by the increasing attention this gland receives by scientists. The unknown functions of this gland and the search for thymus hormones spur the investigator on and on. In 1962 a great discovery of the role of the thymus was announced—the control of the body's all important immunity mechanism. This is the body's ability to defend itself against infection by bacteria and against the invasion of foreign substances incompatible with its wellbeing. This immunity mechanism impedes the transplantation of organs, causing the body to reject organs not its own as foreign substances. The failure of many recent kidney transplants has been linked with the action of the thymus gland.

More knowledge of the thymus may open the door to transplantation of organs from non-related individuals. It could lead to depositories or banks of various organs similar to the present blood and eye banks. Although as yet no thymus hormones have been discovered, such findings would be of great significance to mankind.

The Adrenals—Glands of Survival

Why should a child not quite ten years old have well-developed muscles, broad shoulders, abundant pubic hair, and large genital organs? Why should a woman have a mustache, a low-pitched manly voice, and hips narrower than her shoulders? Why should some men constantly fight and slug their way against man and nature? When the adrenal glands get out of kilter, there are other manifestations no less startling that gravely disturb the happy course of human lives.

The adrenal glands—there are usually two—are located just above the kidneys. Usually they are in size and shape similar to a large bean. The two adrenals weigh about ten grams—as much as two five cent pieces. Structurally the adrenal is only about one quarter of an inch thick. It spreads at its broadest point to a width of about two inches. There are two distinct parts —an outside *cortex* or bark, and a soft pulpy center known as the *medulla*. The adrenal glands are supplied with an inordinately large blood supply. They secrete adrenalin from the medulla and cortisone from the cortex—each a boon to mankind.

Excessive secretions of the adrenal medulla will produce an excess of pep. In excessive secretions of the cortex there will be sex precocity. The cortex appears to stimulate sex gland growth and to bring on sexual maturity. A normal, balanced endocrine system helps a person develop according to his or her genetic sexual structure.

Living organisms from microbes to men have self-adjusting systems. The many internal activities of the living organisms are regulated to keep the internal system as a whole functioning at a nearly constant level. This is accomplished mainly through the hormones of the adrenals under control of the pituitary. The adrenals help the body remain in a state of inner balance. It could well be that the familiar saying, "a man is as old as his arteries," will be replaced by "a man is as old as his adrenals."

The Pancreas, Insulin, and Diabetes

Whenever the word *insulin* is mentioned the mind immediately thinks of *diabetes*. Why isn't the word *pancreas* associated with diabetes or with insulin? It should be. The pancreas is all but forgotten. The magic of insulin—its control of the diabetic's life span—is a fascinating story in which the pancreas plays a major role.

The pancreas is the longest gland in the body—7 to 8 inches in length. It lies in the abdomen beneath the stomach in the curve of the duodenum to which it is firmly attached. It has a short, thick right end that is known as the *head*, which is followed by a thinner and longer part, the *body*, that tapers into a *tail* at the left end. It is yellowish-gray and it has a plentiful blood supply. The *islands of Langerhans* are many thousands of microscopic groups of cells without ducts distributed throughout the pancreas. It is the removal or the destruction of these cells that produces diabetes.

The underlying cause of diabetes is failure of the pancreas to produce enough insulin to control metabolism of the carbohydrate foods. In other words, starch and sugar in food is not burned to yield energy. Before the discovery of insulin in 1921 the standard remedy for diabetes was control of the diet, eliminating sugar, cutting down on starches, restricting carbohydrates. All were employed with varying success.

Impotence and loss of sex desire is one of the common complications of diabetes. Even though the sugar in the system is under control and the blood sugar maintained at something near normal by diet and insulin, the inability to have marital relations is still one of the common complications. It is the direction of the impotence that becomes different—the sexual disability is not the usual weakness of the erection but instead the failure to complete the sexual act by ejaculation. But diabetes does not seem to be a frequent cause of non-fertility in men. This is proven by semen analysis—a valuable means of estimating fertility.

Today with insulin, the many miracle drugs, and a better understanding of diet, there is every possibility that diabetes will not bar a man and wife from a fruitful life. Today diabetes should not be a bar to marriage—today's adult diabetics are normally fertile and can have children.

Studies indicate there is no demonstrable retrogression in thyroid secretory powers with the advancing years. Equally significant information on the activity of the adrenals has been presented to demonstrate well sustained activity and excellent function of the adrenal glands and its hormones even in persons over eighty years old. Although there is a 10 to 20 percent reduction of effective pancreatic activity in the very late years, there is still more than sufficient secretory function. There is essentially normal secretion of pituitary hormones in the eighty-year-old group. This suggests a marked organ reserve. It is apparent that the entire endocrine system is essentially intact and perfectly capable of effective function at any age.

12. Mental Blocks to Successful Sex

SEX IS A SOURCE of great joy for those who control their sexual impulse, harnessing this great force and making it their servant. Yet life should never be wholly centered upon sexuality. The creative impulse can be utilized in other ways and the stress directed into other channels. The suppression of the libido may cause neurotic disturbances and disruptions in our subconscious mind. But it also can do wonderful things in the way of achievement.

Psychic Frigidity

Ruling out physical causes, there is often psychic coldness or frigidity in women. The dominant factor can usually be traced to unfavorable education during which the woman has been conditioned to reject normal sexual intercourse, causing her emotional relations to be decidedly indifferent. This condition is often dissipated, especially in an older woman when her emotions are deeply stirred by genuine love. Finding ardent love, perhaps for the first time, late in life with an understanding man can lead to successful relations that will transform a formerly frigid woman into a responsive warm mate eager for coitus.

The term frigidity can be applied to a woman who cannot arrive at orgasm during intercourse. This may be the result of her attitude toward sex with fear being the basic emotion. Sex ignorance, feelings of guilt, false modesty, nervousness, and tenseness coupled with physical symptoms such as headaches and fatigue contribute to make a woman unresponsive.

Many beautiful women are sexually frigid—they are not capable of giving love—they only want to be admired. Their face is their fortune, they believe. These women are few in number. Many beautiful women are charming, intelligent, and eager to give and share their love.

If there is a change in women's desire it is because of mental or emotional reactions. Some women feel they will be rejected sexually. They convince themselves that this is inevitable and wind up rejecting sex. Then there is the opposite mental reaction—women whose entire married lives have been spent in taking precautions against pregnancy. After the menopause they find themselves suddenly free. For the first time they enjoy the sexual act with complete abandon. Sometimes in this period a woman will marry a much younger man. As a neurotic she is trying to show the world that she is still young and desirable. This type of marriage seldom endures. This type of woman has not learned how to control her emotions and how to make the most of her years gracefully.

It has been noted by many scientists that sexual intercourse is, for a woman, a real psychic panacea. This is true for each and every successful occasion. Intercourse brings out and develops all the latent strength of a woman's character, enriching her sweetness. It provides her with serenity and poise. Each occasion revives and refreshes a woman. This is true both for the young woman and for the woman after menopause. This ties in with the consensus that continency does not increase the span of life; rather, ripe old age is the usual result of an active sex life and a happy marriage.

Doctor William S. Sadler makes this enlightening statement: "There is no human relationship in which so much can be shared, so much of emotional and spiritual value given to each other as in the sexual relationship, if the attitude toward each other as man and wife is normal!"

Women do not move toward frigidity merely as they grow older. The cause is usually deep-seated and of long duration. Frigid women often believe that their lack of sexual feeling is inborn and irremediable. Yet frigidity may be caused by the same factors that create impotence in men.

In assuming responsibilities outside the home, wives place themselves under a strain at least as great as those of their husbands and their sexual vigor may be impaired by the demands of business life. Not many women can work in an office all day, return home to cook and clean, and still be amorous wives. In time they are likely to rebel if their tasks become too difficult, and they may acquire an aversion toward their husbands.

On the other hand, many sexually normal young women have had frigidity forced upon them, perhaps unwillingly. They have been instilled, often unconsciously, with an aversion toward love-making, and conditioned from their earliest years by family quarrels or by a mother miserable in her own marriage who constantly condemns men as "selfish brutes."

A man can know the importance of foreplay to a woman during the sex act. He can approach his wife with tenderness, he can mesh his emotional needs with her—he knows all the answers and techniques—but his wife may not respond. The assumption is that she is frigid. Sexologists believe that there is no such thing as a physically frigid woman. In their experience they never found a woman who is born with nerve inadequacy.

When a man complains that his wife is frigid—that she is as cold as a block of ice—what he really means is that she cannot achieve an orgasm in their intercourse. Physical sex is distasteful to several million women who need sex education to remove their feelings of guilt, or false modesty, and other fears of many kinds. It is the nervous, tense woman who is usually frigid. Rarely is a man so free of his own problems, and, at the same time, so gifted with wisdom and understanding that he is able to display the tact, patience, and tenderness required to overcome his wife's antipathy to sexual relations.

Mental Impotence

When a man physically capable of intercourse discovers that he cannot have an erection or ejaculation, the cause is usually mental. Impotence may be temporary or be a permanent condition—it may be partial or be complete. Sex arousal, ejaculation, and erection are controlled by the nerve impulses reaching the brain and then relayed to the erection-ejaculation center located in the base of the spine. When the erection center sends enough impulses to the penis, there is an erection. When the ejaculation center sends enough impulses to the urethra (where it passes through the prostate), there is ejaculation. These two processes can take place in two ways: (1) in dreams where the involvement is the unconscious mind, or (2) when awake where the conscious mind is at work from sensory impressions, erotic thoughts, and memories. The control of the mind in this part of the sex act is absolute without respect for age.

This relay system must be in perfect working order. Normal sexual response can be disrupted by psychological means, such as fears, rejection, guilt, worry, conflicts, and attitudes. Removal of these mental and emotional factors can contribute to a return of potency and a fulfilling sex life. In the mature man there is sometimes an emotional block that short circuits the impulses to the brain so that erection can be brought about only by physical means. A thorough physical examination will disclose if the impotence is caused by high blood pressure, diabetes, the kidneys, injuries of various kinds, or lack of male hormone.

In mental (psychic) impotence the cause is often due to some past experience that contributed to loss of confidence in his virility. His impotence can be with all women, with some particular woman, or with certain women. It is an idea working below the conscious level—a fear or a sexual taboo so that a man imagines he is sexually incompetent. This feeling is so powerful that it controls his sexual life. It must be remembered that at times many young men experience impotence that is due to psychological causes.

The male, of whatever age, who realizes that "it's all in the mind" is well on the way to conquering this symptom. He must convince himself that he is fully capable of performing the act of coitus. He must train himself in the art of love and practice becoming a lover. He must have positive feelings about himself —he must feel that he can fail in the sex act on occasion, confident that it is only a temporary condition. He cannot have any doubts, any feelings of inadequacy!

Finally, he must have a suitable partner, one that will instill confidence in his ability—one who is not cold and indifferent. He must give all his energy to this end and concentrate on the act, relegating all other thoughts into the background. He must accept the world as it is, letting small worries and vexations roll off his back. All energies and thoughts must be on sex and directed to that end. It is a concentration of the mind in its most intense form.

Some men, normally virile in their relation with one woman, are impotent in the sexual presence of another whom they may desire even more. Over-anxiety to please often produces the same sexual incapacity as indifference.

Premature ejaculation is a problem for men of all ages. Sometimes it is caused by unusual sensitivity of the penis and posterior urethra. Very often mental anxiety can trigger this condition by sending an over-abundance of impulses to the ejaculation center at the base of the spinal cord. Emotional retraining by removing fears, tensions, and anxiety is often successful in overcoming this condition.

Not infrequently a husband's impotence is a refraction of his wife's frigidity. If she is indifferent or even averse to intercourse, the husband is more than likely to develop a feeling of futility and frustration which, in turn, leads to impotence.

Can impotence be caused by abstaining from sexual intercourse? This is a debatable question. When should a man's sexual powers end? This is another debatable question. There are men in their nineties with strong desires leading to erection and ejaculation.

Fears and Mental Conflicts

Fears of various kinds can only hasten the onset of failure in the sex act—fears that nearly always never materialize. The fear of failure in sex relations can alienate a man from his wife. He may at first only change to a separate bed, and then gradually devise many excuses for not approaching his wife. Women also have their fears and they are powerful—fears of losing their husband, fears that they no longer are attractive. That fears have a strong inhibitory influence on the sexual organs is recognized by nearly everyone. It is the hidden fears of sex that are dangerous, such as the fear of ageing prematurely.

It has been estimated that 75 percent of the people who seek medical advice suffer from "nerves." These people are not mentally incompetent. Instead they are almost invariably highly intelligent, idealistic, and mentally alert. Psychoneurosis has therefore been called the disease of the thinker and the dreamer.

It is almost impossible to estimate the variety and the severity of nervous symptoms that result from nothing more or less than some phase of sexual abnormality or repression. All sorts of aches and pains, neuralgia, neuritis, rheumatism, stomach and intestinal disturbances, disturbed heart action, phobias of many kinds have been traced to a faulty or disturbed sex life.

Phobias and Sex

Phobias are intense fears. Nothing in human experience is so unreal as the source of fear. The victim of fear is a problem in himself. He is really trying to solve one group of problems by another set of problems. Here are some of the common phobias that may interfere with sex activity:

Nyctophobia is fear of the dark. Some otherwise normal people cannot have sex relations in a room without a light burning. They are made inordinately nervous by sounds both real and imaginary. The wind, the doors, the windows, the creaking of the floor, all alarm them so effectually as to prevent pleasurable sex relations.

Claustrophobia is the fear of closed places. Some people become nervous and fidgety and sometimes pale with fear when an elevator door closes and they find themselves in a steel cage. When in other tight places, they find breathing difficult, cold perspiration breaks out on the face, and they have a suffocating feeling. During the sex act a woman suffering from claustrophobia cannot bear to have the male on top of her in the dominant position. She feels suffocated, confined, restricted. She must change positions to be the dominant one—to lie on top of her male partner.

Microphobia is the fear of germs, and *Mysophobia* is the fear of dirt. Both can affect sexual intercourse. People with these phobias fear to shake hands with anyone. They are afraid to kiss. Although their sexual partners may wash their hands over and over again, they cannot allow them to touch their sex organs.

Agoraphobia is the fear of open spaces. Before engaging in coitus people with this phobia must see where the bed is placed. It cannot be in the middle of a room, it must be in a corner with the head against a wall, which is the most sheltered position.

Aerophobia is the fear of air. Many people fear winds and have strong feelings about drafts. They will close all the windows and doors before engaging in coitus, which often works a hardship on their partner who cannot stand being in a stuffy room. One of this couple must give in or there will be no intercourse.

Zoophobia is the fear of animals. It is impossible for these individuals to engage in coitus if there is a cat or dog or other animal in the room. They are afraid the animal might jump on the bed. They cannot stand having the animal watching the performance. Removing the animal will insure a satisfactory sexual experience.

Phobophobia is the fear of fear. Many times nervous people wake up to the realization that they are victims of fear, slaves to their various dreads. Even though they break themselves of many of these phobias, they continue to live in constant fear of fear.

There is a positive method of eliminating fear. Learn exactly what is feared. This may sound utterly simple, but it is true. Ignorance breeds fears and our fears are perpetuated by our own blind spots that prevent the proper appraisal of our phobias. Admit just what it is that you fear—this will lead to a more fulfilling sex life for men and women in any age bracket.

13. Food for Sex Happiness

Legend has it that oysters, clams, and other seafoods can rouse the sex urge. Although the chemical contents of these inhabitants of the sea show no constituent unusual enough to cause potency, the legend has such power of suggestion that a man can be so influenced if he firmly believes a dish of seafood aids him sexually. Crayfish soup is highly reputed to promote the libido and heads the list in the haute cuisine with caviar a close second.

Many men eat eggs as a sexual restorative. Their reputation in this direction is world wide. The yolk has been recommended as being especially invigorating. Eggs in all forms—raw, in alcoholic drinks, in food, in pastry—have been recommended by the sexologists of every nation.

Both eggs and oysters give quick energy. They are light on the stomach, and they do benefit the organism as good food.

Condiments are believed to be of value in the excitation of powerful erotic feelings. Mentioned in erotic literature and in cook books are saffron, cinnamon, vanilla, pepper, peppermint, and ginger from the far East.

In man's ceaseless pursuit of sensual pleasure, fruit has been woven into the literature of erotic cookery. From all parts of the world every edible fruit has been glorified as a sensory stimulant. Among the fruits so honored are apples, apricots, cherries, dates, figs, bananas, peaches, grapes, and pineapples.

Nearly every article of food has at some time been associated with sex life. Either with the genitalia—looking like or smelling like the sex organs—or with some other part of the body, such as the breasts, legs, or buttocks.

As an aid to sexual communion, alcohol, coffee or tea can animate to a small degree especially if imbibed in very limited quantities.

The use of cantharides and oil of peppermint as aphrodisiacs was first mentioned in the writing of Aristotle. Cantharides, obtained from a beetle known as Spanish Fly (an insect found in southern Europe) was used in the eighteenth century as a sexual stimulant. It was cooked in pastry, inserted in candies, and was used by Madame de Pompadour in her efforts to regain the love of Louis XV.

Nux vomica, strychnine, cocaine, and hashish can produce erotic potency in the brain. Yohimbine goads the nerves of the spinal column, resulting in a stimulation of the genitalia. The drug adrenaline has been tried by men looking for a perfect aphrodisiac. It is claimed to have effects similar to ephedrine and benzedrine. All these drugs carry warning labels. They are dangerous and must not be used except under the supervision of a skilled physician—who will not as a rule prescribe them for potency problems.

Honey is a frequent ingredient in Oriental dishes that are to be served as aphrodisiacs. Galen, court physician to Emperor Marcus Aurelius, recommended a glass of honey as a sex stimulant to be taken before bedtimes, together with almonds and grains of the pine tree. Avicenna, a thirteenth century physician, recommended for the same purpose a combination of honey, pepper, and ginger. Hippocrates, the ancient physician of 400 B.C., prescribed honey as a help for a long and happy life. It is not known if he meant a long sex life.

The only sweetness available to man for many ages was honey made by bees from flower nectars. Although there have been many sweetening substitutes manufactured through the years, there still is only one sweet that offers life-giving qualities and that is honey from the bee.

It is only in recent years that the discovery was made that numerous minerals are needed by the body in tiny amounts. The normal individual will find in honey all the necessary minerals and in the right quantities—iron, copper, manganese, silica, chlorine, and so on. Honey has been found to contain all the vitamins necessary to health.

Cane sugar and starches must undergo a process of inversion in the gastrointestinal tract to convert them into simple sugars. Honey, being predigested by the bee, eliminates the need for the human gastrointestinal tract to perform this additional labor. Therefore it is quickly absorbed into the blood stream, providing a quick release of energy.

Physicians now advise the addition of honey to the diet for better muscular tone, as a sedative to the nervous system, and to improve the function of the heart muscle. With the prevalence of cardiovascular diseases this is an important factor. Honey will, by its several effects, render old age more enjoyable. It is suggested as a remedy for insomnia. A tablespoon of honey has been advised by some authorities for people having difficulty in falling asleep or for those who wake up during the night and then find it difficult to fall asleep again. It is worth a trial. Explore the many wonderful honey flavors—thyme from Hymettus, Tupelo from Florida, or orange blossom from California. Energy is what everyone desires—honey will supply that food energy for the athlete and for the lover!

Even so, the fact remains that a balanced diet will in the long run do more to prolong life and provide the energy needed for active sex than will any single food. But combining the many varied foodstuffs available in this country to give the older generation health, longevity, and an enjoyable sex life is an art. Many variables must be weighed, considered, and brought into focus.

The problem is not simple—construct a diet that will supply

the necessary calories, vitamins, minerals, amino-acids, fats, carbohydrates, and proteins according to a person's age, sex, height, weight, and activity. Consideration also should be given to the climate and the environment in which he lives. All the elements together must supply energy for the sex life—for the daily pursuit of happiness. In the search for a perfect diet the intake must (1) furnish heat and energy, (2) build and repair tissue, and (3) regulate body processes.

Proteins provide one of these necessary ingredients—they build and repair tissue. Protein is found in meat, fish, poultry, eggs, cheese, milk, legumes (dried beans and peas), peanut butter, and nuts. Proteins are found in all vegetables except radishes, rhubarb, and watercress—but don't eliminate these three from the diet because they do supply vitamins and minerals. Among the vegetable kingdom the best source of proteins are potatoes, almonds, cocoanuts, fresh green peas, fresh lima beans and soy beans. Many fruits also aid in supplying the proteins, among them are apricots, bananas, blackberries, grapes, peaches, muskmelons, raspberries, and strawberries.

Proteins are the least fattening of foods and they are the one food element that is indispensable. Almost all parts of the body are made principally from protein substances. One gram of protein yields about 4.1 calories. A man weighing 154 pounds requires about 70 grams of protein a day. A woman of 128 pounds requires about 58 grams of protein daily. Some people have the impression that less protein is needed by older people. But, according to a recent recommendation of the Food and Nutrition Board, the person aged sixty-five has the same protein requirement as the person aged twenty-five!

Quickly and easily assimilated, carbohydrates are the chief sources of energy for muscle, brain, and nerve tissue. They aid the oxidation or burning of fats. Carbohydrate sources are bread and cereals, potatoes and corn, dried fruits, sweetened fruits, sugar, syrup, jelly, jam, and honey. They are tempting to the palate, so overindulgence in candies, jams, and other sweet food is quite common. They are the major source of calories for all people. The energy from one pound of carbohydrates equals 1,807 calories.

The third class of nutrients are the fats—that dread word for the obese man or woman. Fat is found in butter and cream, in salad oils and dressings, in cooking fats, and in fat meats. Authorities agree that only from 20 to 30 percent of our diet should consist of fats and not the 40 percent and over now consumed. This means cutting fats by approximately one-half. Fats are valuable as a source of heat and are the most compact forms of stored energy. One pound of fat furnishes nearly 4,000 calories. The daily fat requirement for a person is about 100 grams. Fats form a padding to protect the vital organs of the body and serve as insulation to retain body heat. Try to memorize the fats in some common foods—the invisible fats, such as almonds that are three-quarter fat and avocado that is one-quarter fat. Other fat foods are chocolate, cocoanut, cream, egg yolk, cheese, haddock, halibut, herring, and lamb.

Vitamins are another indispensable element in foods. Their presence in the food you eat is a fundamental essential to health and well-being. We cannot live without vitamins! Nutritional improvement with the proper vitamins can result in a marked increase in libido and sexeual potency.

Vitamin E is called the sex vitamin. It is claimed to help restore virility to a man, assist a woman to conceive, and promote sexual desire between man and woman. Vitamin E keeps the reproductive organs in good condition. A severe vitamin E deficiency may cause sterility. In the female a vitamin E deficiency does not affect her gonads, but damage is done to her maturing embryo, perhaps causing abortion. In the male a deficiency may cause the sperm to degenerate and then vanish. It has been found that Vitamin E nourishes the tissues of the body, rejuvenating both the muscles and the skin. It may also affect potency but this remains to be proven.

Vitamin E is included in some combination vitamin capsules

—but not in all. Vitamin E is found in seedgerm oil—wheat germ ol is an especially rich source. It is also found in corn oil, cottonseed oil, and in lettuce, spinach, watercress, and other leafy greens. There is considerable Vitamin E in milk, butter, eggs, fat, meat, and liver. Because of its wide distribution there is small chance of a vitamin E deficiency in any balanced diet, particularly as this vitamin is very resistant to heat, light, drying, distillation, cooking, and oxidation. Moreover, it is hoarded abundantly in muscle and fat.

The latest discovery about vitamin E is its power to assist and strengthen the heart. Victims of some heart ailments have recovered when their vitamin E deficiency was corrected. Deficiency can also cause inflammation of nerve and muscle tissues.

A certain minimum amount of vitamin E is necessary—an abundance will not produce wonders and will not accomplish more than the minimum requirement for healthy body functioning. Many of the diets advocated for rejuvenation, virility, potency, and vitality are built with this vitamin as the cornerstone.

But it must be emphasized that all the vitamins are essential to glandular health. A lack of any can quickly have a marked effect on the sex glands. Vitamins are essential to the health of both the ovaries and the testicles contributing to normal sex interest in both men and women.

Here is a listing of foods that contain various vitamins. Vegetables are listed in detail, the thought being to spur the American to turn to vegetables in greater variety. The choice is wide. Remember that vitamins alone cannot take the place of food under any circumstances!

Vitamin A is supplied by the following vegetables and fruits: parsley, Hubbard squash, sweet potato, carrot, pumpkin, cabbage, peaches, escarole, spinach, kale, broccoli, apricots, chard, string beans, avocado, asparagus, beet tops, collards, endive, okra, green pepper, tomato, lettuce, mustard and turnip greens, oranges, pineapple, and soy beans. Milk, liver, eggs, kidney, fish, cheese are splendid sources of vitamin A.

Vitamin B_1 (thiamin) is supplied by the following vegetables and fruits: fresh lima beans, avocado, asparagus, cauliflower, parsnips, oranges, carrots, apricots, almonds, artichokes, sprouts, beet greens, broccoli, cabbage, collards, kale, sweet and white potatoes, lettuce, eggplant, okra, tomato, turnips, watercress, cantaloupe, bananas, dates, figs, grapes, grapefruit, apples, pears, pineapple, raisins, raspberries and watermelon. Other sources are liver, fish, eggs, milk, meat, enriched breads and cereals, poultry, and dried yeast.

Vitamin B_2 (riboflavin) is supplied by the following: turnips, greens, fresh lima beans, broccoli, apricots, dried peaches, collards, endive, escarole, kale, greens, watercress, asparagus, sprouts, cabbage, carrots, cauliflower, beets, eggplant, sweet potato, white potato, tomato, soy beans, avocado, raisins, banana, grapefruit, pears, melons, peaches, figs, apples, meat, eggs, dairy products, milk, kidney, heart, dried yeast, and whole wheat and enriched white breads.

Vitamin C (ascorbic acid) is supplied by the following: peppers, broccoli, greens, kohlrabi, cauliflower, watercress, lemons, oranges, grapefruit, tangerines, melons, cabbage, papaya, banana, strawberries, rhubarb, tomatoes, turnips, asparagus, fresh lima beans, radishes, fresh peas, lettuce, endive, potato, apples, onions, celery, and carrots.

Vitamin D is the sunshine vitamin. Sunlight activates the bone building mechanism by stimulating the skin to manufacture its own vitamin D. It is supplied also by eggs, butter, herring, sardines, tuna, salmon, shrimp, and liver.

Vitamin K is supplied by the following: cabbage, kale, cauliflower, spinach, all green vegetables, tomatoes, liver, pork, oats, soy beans, and wheat bran.

Vitamin P is supplied by the citrus gruits.

Vitamin B_6 is supplied by meat, fish, liver, yeast, grains, and many vegetables.

Vitamin B_{12} is supplied by lean meat, liver, eggs, dairy products, kidney, milk, oysters, fish, and soy beans.

Niacin (nicotinic acid) is found in beef, lamb, pork, fish, poultry, liver, peanuts, whole wheat, and enriched wheat products.

Folic acid is found in green vegetables, liver, kidney, and in yeast.

If the vitamins in the diet are adequate, swallowing more vitamin capsules will have little or no effect. Except for the rate of absorption, the vitamin problem of the senior citizen is the same as that for the young person.

The energy-producing or heat value of food is measured in

DESIRABLE WEIGHTS

(Courtesy of Metropolitan Life Insurance Company)
Weight in Pounds According to Frame (In Indoor Clothing)

	HEIGHT (with shoes on) 1-inch heels Feet	Inches	SMALL FRAME	MEDIUM FRAME	LARGE FRAME
Men	5	2	112–120	118–129	126–141
of Ages 25	5	3	115–123	121–133	129–144
and Over	5	4	118–126	124–136	132–148
	5	5	121–129	127–139	135–152
	5	6	124–133	130–143	138–156
	5	7	128–137	134–147	142–161
	5	8	132–141	138–152	147–166
	5	9	136–145	142–156	151–170
	5	10	140–150	146–160	155–174
	5	11	144–154	150–165	159–179
	6	0	148–158	154–170	164–184
	6	1	152–162	158–175	168–189
	6	2	156–167	162–180	173–194
	6	3	160–171	167–185	178–199
	6	4	164–175	172–190	182–204

terms of calories—one calorie being the amount of heat required to raise the temperature of one liter of water one degree centigrade. At age 25 a man weighing 154 pounds and 5' 9" tall will require 3,200 calories daily. Office workers and those in sedentary positions will require less. At age 45 this same man will require only 3,000 calories. And at age 65 the calorie requirement falls to 2,500! A similar condition applies to women. At 25 a woman weighing 128 pounds and 5' 4" tall needs 2,300 calories daily. At age 45 this same woman will require only 2,200 calories. But at age 65 she will only need 1,800 calories. These caloric needs should be supplied by 15 percent protein, 25 percent fats and 60 percent carbohydrates. This will give the approximate proportions for a successful diet.

Here is a chart for men and women showing desirable weights according to a person's height and body frame.

	HEIGHT (with shoes on) 2-inch heels		SMALL	MEDIUM	LARGE
	Feet	Inches	FRAME	FRAME	FRAME
Women	4	10	92– 98	96–107	104–119
of Ages 25	4	11	94–101	98–110	106–122
and Over	5	0	96–104	101–113	109–125
	5	1	99–107	104–116	112–128
	5	2	102–110	107–119	115–131
	5	3	105–113	110–122	118–134
	5	4	108–116	113–126	121–138
	5	5	111–119	116–130	125–142
	5	6	114–123	120–135	129–146
	5	7	118–127	124–139	133–150
	5	8	122–131	128–143	137–154
	5	9	126–135	132–147	141–158
	5	10	130–140	136–151	145–163
	5	11	134–144	140–155	149–168
	6	0	138–148	144–159	153–173

For girls between 18 and 25, subtract 1 pound for each year under 25.

The human body requires calories whether awake or asleep. Here is a tabulation of the number of calories per hour expended by a man who weighs 154 pounds in various situations.

Sleeping	65
Awake (lying still)	77
Sitting	100
Dressing and undressing	118
Reading	120
Typing rapidly	140
Laundry (light)	161
Sweeping	169
Walking (moderate)	300
Walking downstairs	364
Sawing wood	460
Swimming	500
Walking upstairs	1100

Below is a list of some everyday foods and their calorie value. These figures are from the Institute of Home Economics, Agricultural Research Service, U.S. Department of Agriculture.

Apple, 1 large, fresh, 3″ in dia.	117
Apple pie, ⅙ of a 9″ pie	377
Applesauce, sweetened, ½ cup	92
Apricots, 3 whole, fresh	60
Asparagus soup, cream, 1 cup	160
Avocado, ½ medium	275
Bacon, 1 crisp 6″ strip	48
Banana, 1 medium size	130
Beans, baked, canned, ½ cup	162
Beans, green, ½ cup cooked	13
Beef, corned, hash, ½ cup	145
Beef, hamburger, 1 large patty	300
Beefsteak, sirloin, 3 oz.	300
Beef tongue, 3 slices	160
Beer, 1 glass, 8 oz.	115
Biscuit, baking powder	130

Blueberries, fresh, ¾ cup	64
Bologna sausage, 1 slice	66
Bread, commercial rye, 1 slice	50
Bread, commercial, white, 1 slice	60
Bread, commercial, whole wheat, 1 slice	55
Butter, 1 pat, ¼ in.	50
Cabbage, ½ cup, raw	10
Cake, chocolate layer, 2" square	356
Cake, coffee, 1 piece	133
Cantaloupe, ½ of 4" melon	30
Carrot, 1 whole, raw, small	20
Celery soup, cream, 1 cup	200
Cheese, American, 1" cube	79
Cheese, cottage, ½ cup	100
Cheese, cream, 1½ oz.	159
Cheese, Swiss, 1 oz.	105
Cherries, canned, sweetened, ½ cup	100
Chicken, broiler, ½ medium	125
Chicken, fried, ½ breast	232
Chicken salad, ½ cup	200
Chocolate, 1 cup made with milk	277
Chocolate bar, milk, 1 oz.	154
Chocolate ice cream, ½ cup	180
Clam chowder, Manhattan, 1 cup	87
Codfish balls, 1 of 2" diameter	100
Coffee, clear, 1 cup	0
Cola beverages, 8 oz.	105
Corn bread, 1 2" square	139
Corn flakes, ¾ cup	62
Corn on cob, 1 medium	92
Cracker, soda 1 2½ in. square	24
Cream of wheat, cooked, ¾ cup	100
Custard pie, ⅙ of 9" pie	266
Doughnut, plain, one	135
Egg, 1 fried in 1 tsp. butter	105
Farina, ¾ cup cooked	100
Frankfurter, one	125

French dressing, 1 tbsp.	59
Gingerbread, 2″ square	200
Grapefruit, ½ medium	70
Griddle cakes, 2 4″ in dia.	150
Halibut steak, 3″	125
Ham, baked, 4½ x 4. ½ slice	400
Honey, 1 tablespoon	62
Ice cream, plain ½ cup	100
Jam or jelly, 1 tbsp.	60
Lamb chop, broiled ¾″ thick	175
Lemonade, 1 cup	100
Lemon meringue pie, ⅙ of 9″ pie	280
Lentil soup, 1 cup	606
Lettuce, iceberg, ¼ head	18
Liver, beef, fried 2 slices 3″	175
Liverwurst, 1 slice 3″ dia.	80
Macaroni and cheese, ½ cup	300
Malted milk, 8 oz.	270
Maple syrup, 1 tbsp.	50
Margarine, 1 tbsp.	100
Mayonnaise, 1 tbsp.	109
Meat loaf, beef and pork, 1 slice	264
Milk, skimmed, 1 cup	88
Milk, whole, fresh, 1 cup	166
Muffin, English, 1 large	280
Noodles, egg, cooked, ½ cup	100
Oatmeal, cooked, ½ cup	75
Onions, creamed, ⅓ cup	100
Orange, 1 average size	75
Orange juice, 1 cup	100
Pancake, 1 4″ dia.	75
Peach, fresh, 1 large	50
Peanut butter, 1 tbsp.	90
Pear, fresh, 1 medium size	60
Peas, canned, ½ cup	73
Pineapple, canned, 1 slice and juice	78
Plums, fresh, 4	100

Food	Calories
Popcorn, 1½ cups, no butter	100
Pork chop, 3" x 5" x 1"	290
Pork tenderloin, 2 oz.	200
Potato, baked, 1 medium size	90
Potato, sweet, baked, medium size	155
Potato, French fried, 10 pieces	155
Prune juice, 1 cup	170
Pumpkin pie, ⅙ of 9" pie	300
Rhubarb, fresh, 1 cup diced	137
Rice, white cooked, ½ cup	100
Roll, hard, white, 1 average size	95
Salmon, canned, ½ cup	206
Sardines, canned, 4 large	100
Sauerkraut, ⅔ cup	27
Sausage, pork link, 3" x ½"	94
Shredded wheat biscuit, 1 large	100
Shrimp, fried, 4 large	259
Sirup, corn, 1 tbsp.	57
Spaghetti, plain, cooked, 1 cup	218
Spinach, cooked, chopped, ½ cup	23
Split pea soup, 1 cup	268
Strawberries, fresh, ⅓ cup	30
Sugar, granulated, 1 tbsp.	50
Tapioca pudding, ½ cup	133
Tea, clear, unsweetened, 1 cup	0
Tomato juice, 1 cup	50
Tuna fish, canned in oil, ½ cup	300
Turkey, roast, light meat, 4" x 4" x ¾"	183
Turnips, cooked, 1 cup	40
Veal cutlet, breaded, average serving	217
Waffles, 1 5½" dia.	232
Watermelon, 1 slice, ¾ x 6"	90
Yogurt, whole milk, ½ cup	83
Zwieback, 1 slice	35

Now that the calorie allowances have been determined for the weight, height and age of a person and the calories in many foods have been listed, simple arithmetic should enable you to find a satisfactory balanced diet.

Here is a normal diet for people over sixty.

Breakfast	Lunch	Dinner
1 piece of any fruit or several prunes or figs, or fruit juice ½ cup of any cereal with sugar and milk, or 2 eggs, any style. 1 slice of bread or toast with ½ pat of butter. Tea, coffee or milk (sugar and milk may be taken with tea or coffee)	1 meat or egg sandwich, or any meat, fish, vegetable or fruit salad, or 1 portion of meat. 1 or 2 vegetables 1 slice of bread. 1 piece of fruit or canned fruit, stewed fruit, etc. 1 glass of milk, tea or coffee.	1 portion of meat, fowl or fish. 1 or 2 vegetables. Green salad. 1 or 2 slices of bread. Dessert: fruit, cake, pie, ice cream, etc. Tea, coffee or milk.

(a total of about eight glasses of liquids should be consumed during each twenty-four hours)

To aid in the construction and planning of the menu, three samples are next listed, courtesy of the Metropolitan Life Insurance Company.

NO. 1—A 1,000 CALORIE DAILY DIET

Breakfast:
Fresh fruit or juice	1 serving—½ cup
Egg—cooked without fat	1
or	
Cereal	1 small serving
Bread	1 slice
Butter or margarine	1 level teaspoon
Skim milk or buttermilk	1 glass—6 ounces
Clear coffee or tea	

Dinner:
Lean meat, fish or poultry	3 ounces (cooked)
Vegetables (raw or cooked)	½ cup cooked; raw, freely
Skim milk or buttermilk	1 glass—6 ounces
Fruit (raw, cooked or canned without sugar)	1 serving—½ cup

Lunch or Supper:
Cottage cheese or lean meat	½ cup of cheese or 2 ounces of meat
Vegetables (raw or cooked)	½ cup cooked; raw, freely
Skim milk or buttermilk	1 glass, 6 ounces
Fruit (raw, cooked or canned without sugar)	1 serving—½ cup

NO. 2—A 1,200 CALORIE DAILY DIET

Breakfast:
Fresh fruit or juice	1 serving—½ cup
Egg, cooked without fat, or	1
Cereal	1 small serving
Bread	1 slice
Butter or margarine	1 level teaspoon
Skim milk	1 glass—6 ounces
Clear coffee or tea	

Dinner:
Lean meat, fish, or poultry	4 ounces (cooked)
Vegetables (raw or cooked)	½ cup cooked; raw, freely
Potato or bread	1 small potato or 1 slice bread
Butter or margarine	1 level teaspoon
Skim milk	1 glass—6 ounces
Fruit (raw, cooked or canned without sugar)	1 serving—½ cup

Lunch or Supper:
Cottage cheese or lean meat	½ cup of cheese or 2 ounces of meat
Vegetables (raw or cooked)	½ cup cooked; raw, freely

Skim milk   1 glass—6 ounces
Fruit (raw, cooked or canned
    without sugar)   1 serving—½ cup

NO. 3—A 1,500 CALORIE DAILY DIET
Breakfast:
Fresh fruit or juice   1 serving—½ cup
Egg—cooked without fat   1
or
Cereal   1 serving of cereal (1 cup,
                                             prepared or ½ cup cooked)
Bread   1 slice
Butter or margarine   1 level teaspoon
Skim milk   1 cup—8 ounces
Coffee or tea
Cream   1 tablespoon

Dinner:
Lean meat, fish or poultry   4 ounces (cooked)
Vegetables (raw or cooked)   ½ cup cooked; raw, freely
Potato   1 small
Butter or margarine   1 level teaspoon
Skim milk   1 cup—8 ounces
Fruit (raw, cooked or canned
    without sugar)   1 serving—½ cup

Lunch or Supper:
Cottage cheese or lean meat   ½ cup of cheese or 2 ounces of
                                             meat
Vegetables (raw or cooked)   ½ cup cooked
Bread   1 slice
Butter or margarine   1 level teaspoon
Skim milk   1 cup—8 ounces
Fruit, plain custard or plain cookies   ½ cup of fruit or custard, or
                                             2 cookies

Wise men and women pick and choose the food that agrees with their stomachs and eat neither too much nor too little. The general rule that might profitably be adopted is to rise from the table with a feeling that there is still more room for food, instead of a stuffed, stupefying, uncomfortable logginess. Other things being equal, the moderate eater who rises from the table feeling that the last word has not yet been said to his stomach will get up for a good many years longer than the person who is kinder to his appetite than to himself.

Natural and not artificially goaded appetite should tell when to eat. Depending upon a person's constitution, waiting to eat when hungry is not always the best of advice. For some people to wait until Nature signals that she wants fuel for her furnace is not always a dependable sign. For many people, eating more than three meals daily can be beneficial—five or six small meals might be just the thing. Others can thrive on two moderate meals.

It has been known for many years that proper diet is the keystone for the continuance of sexual function. When a person suffers nutritional deficiency he also has impaired sexual activity. Virility can be prolonged and old age can be postponed with a correct diet.

14. Sex and the Overweight

In the obese, sexual capacity becomes limited. The skin's heat-regulating mechanism is thrown out of kilter because fat is a poor conductor of heat. There is an uneven distribution of blood supply that predisposes the skin to eruptions, eczema, carbuncles, and boils. Increase in the surface of the blood-vessel network places a strain upon the heart. There is an encroachment of fat upon the lungs and diaphragm, hampering normal respiration.

The amount of food a person consumes must be shared by the energy-producing mechanism and the tissue-building mechanism. When the amount of food taken into the body exceeds the amount required for assimilation, then the unused balance is stored as fat. It's that simple!

Statistics show that the obese do not live as long as the thin person. On the average a thin person in good health will live longer than the obese person because the obese are more apt to develop diseases and infections. In order for people to stay in their prime physically and sexually, the appetite must be curtailed. This applies to younger people who will become obese if they eat more than required to maintain their normal body weight.

Often many older persons fall into the habit of eating the

Sex and the Overweight / 111

same quantity of food as they did when much younger—when they were more active. An active young man may need over 3,000 calories for his age, height, and weight. The man over sixty may require only 2,000 calories. This depends on activity. A very active man over sixty may require the same amount of calories as the younger man. A rule stressed by insurance companies and many doctors is that men or women should continue to weigh all through life the same as in their prime—the same as they did between ages 25 and 30.

Over one-fourth of the male adults in the United States eat more than necessary to maintain their normal weight and become fat. And 60 percent of American women become fat as the years roll by.

A woman should concentrate on preserving her figure, because it is her figure that in the long run will stimulate a man's sexual desire. A woman's appearance will be enhanced if she cuts down on her food intake and selects each item with common sense. Time spent putting on her face might be more rewardingly spent on attaining a better figure.

Once past the mid-twenties or early thirties, as men and women gradually gain weight, the fat may slow down their sex drive. The fat man becomes lethargic—he soon lacks eagerness for sexual intercourse. The fat man or woman seldom has a satisfactory sex life. He or she is not interested in physical exertion. Sexual intercourse does require physical exertion, causing the fat person to have fewer and fewer sexual contacts. When both husband and wife are obese, coitus usually becomes onerous!

Reaching a partner in intercourse is a problem for the obese. The wife soon stops trying to cause an erection when her husband is too obese to reach her. Conversely, the husband might have an erection but cannot reach his wife if she is obese.

Here the sexual position becomes important. Various positions must be tried by the obese so that the act will be confortable and require little physical exertion.

Three positions are outlined that should aid the obese in attaining a satisfactory sexual relationship.

(1) The man stands during the act with the woman sitting on the edge of the bed or couch. She stretches the upper part of her body back as far as possible but without lying on her back. Her legs, parted slightly, hang down. If her legs do not reach the floor, some article or furniture must give her support, because her legs must rest on a firm foundation. The man stands between the woman's legs, bending forward and resting his hands on either side of his partner. In this position it is important that the woman should not raise her legs. Depth of penetration can be controlled to some extent by the woman. It will not be deep in this position unless she inclines too far back. If the bed is too low for connection, pillows can be used to raise the woman to the necessary height.

(2) The man may either lie or sit down for this astride position. The woman adopts a straddling position. In this face to face attitude with the man lying down, he keeps his legs slightly bent and the woman sits on him and leans back against his thighs. In this position the woman assumes the active role. Once the penis has been introduced into the vagina, the woman lets herself down until she is sitting on the man with her legs outside of the man. He need not make any motions at all. The woman sits upright and raises and lowers her body rhythmically until culmination is attained. This method yields exceptionally acute sensations and often provides the summit of voluptuous enjoyment for both partners. Penetration is at its deepest. This position is also suitable when the man is tired or lacking in sexual vigour, since it is the woman who plays the active role. A half-erect penis will remain in position when this attitude is adopted since it cannot slip out of the vagina. This position should not be adopted where the woman's vagina is short.

(3) This is similar to the previous position except that the woman's back is toward the male. It can be varied by the woman resting on her hands and knees. In this attitude penetration is

Sex and the Overweight / 113

slight. In this position the woman controls the degree of penetration.

Side positions may be still more comfortable. Supporting the weight of a partner will be eliminated and physical exertion will be held to a minimum.

Every fat person wants to know the best way to reduce. Will it be diet, exercise, or a combination of both? Many people believe that lack of exercise causes double chins and large waistlines. This has been disproved by scientific investigation.

To work off the energy furnished by just one caramel, it will be necessary to walk a mile. One small doughnut or a few pretzels will supply the energy to climb to the top of a tall building. A banana split can be walked off in about seven miles, an ordinary candy bar in five miles. Ingesting 2,500 calories more than necessary requires a thirty-mile walk or run to work off these excess calories! It must be quite evident that exercise by itself will not take off excess poundage. There must be an easier way. And there is—weight control by diet! Realize that weight reduction is in itself not a mystery.

First, find out the calorie value of a few common foods. A list has been compiled in the previous chapter for many popular items.

Second, estimate your present calorie intake. This is best accomplished by charting your food consumption for three days, including all meals, all snacks, and all midnight raids on the refrigerator. Now add up the three-day total of calories. To arrive at the daily average simply divide the total by three. Be honest—don't cheat. Now compare the average daily total with your requirements.

Third, discover how many calories you need for your height, age, and whether for an active person or a sedentary one. An estimate can be made by multiplying your ideal weight by 18. As an example, if your ideal weight should be 130 pounds, then the ideal number of calories should be about 2,340!

Fourth, go back to the chart that has been made from the

three days of observation. Write down the calories that have been supplied by food, and subtract the calorie requirements for basic needs. This will show the number of extra calories consumed beyond absolute needs.

Finally, eliminate the excess calories, and the road is clear for sensible weight reduction.

Reducing without starvation is possible and pleasant. It is a simple matter to lose more by eliminating the high calorie foods. Often the items that appeal and the items that make eating enjoyable need not be entirely eliminated but the size of the portions can be reduced. Cut the piece of pie in half; break the candy bar in half; eat one half of a roll instead of the entire roll. It is not *what* is ingested but the *amount* that counts!

Here is a sample diet for overweight people.

Breakfast	*Lunch*	*Dinner*
Orange juice or ½ grapefruit (no sugar)	Vegetable, meat, fish or fruit salad with juice of lemon and/or vinegar, or 1 portion of lean meat	1 portion of broiled or boiled lean meat, fish or fowl
1 boiled egg		
1 slice toast		2 vegetables such as: spinach, lettuce, tomato, celery, cucumber, cabbage, onion, peppers, asparagus, string beans, etc.
1 cup of tea or coffee with saccharin and milk	Dessert: 1 portion of fresh fruit or low-sugar canned fruit	
	Tea, coffee with saccharin and skimmed milk	Dessert: Jello, fresh or stewed fruit
		Tea, coffee or skimmed milk

Avoid: Bread, rolls, crackers, butter, cream, cheese, beans, potato, noodles, spaghetti, cereals, nuts, cake, pie, pastry, ice cream, candy, gravies, sauces, fried foods, meat fats!

Several times yearly newspapers feature stories of men who have completed long fasts of thirty to forty days. At the conclusion these men claim to be cured of several distressing conditions—usually of many years standing. These stories usually say that only water was consumed during these long fasts and that the fasters felt strong after the long ordeals. Consider! If men are cured of many ailments by fasting, why not try it for over-weight—thereby shedding a lot of excess poundage quickly?

But, the fact is, the absolute fast is seldom successful for obesity. Records show that most people start to gain back poundage after the fast. Many return to their previous weight. Many become heavier. Few can maintain their reduced weight level.

Instead of the lengthy absolute fast for many days, it might be well for the senior citizen to set aside one day a week for a *juice day*. During this twenty-four-hour period only fruit juices would be consumed—orange, apple, grapefruit, tomato, and grape juice. A can of pineapple juice (without sugar) will add variety. This once a week juice day gives the advantages of the absolute fast while at the same time supplying plenty of energy. Such a juice day gently ties in with the Bible admonition—work six days and rest the seventh. The juice day rests the organs a full twenty-four hours, giving the digestive system repose every seventh day.

A *fruit day* is a variation of the same idea. Eat only fresh fruit for a twenty-four hour period. This is most practical in the spring, summer and early fall when the markets display a great variety of fruit. All fruit is splendid for regular elimination—an aid in cleansing the system of poisonous wastes.

A *vegetable-juice day* will supply needed vitamins, minerals, and salts contained in the vegetables. This helps quick assimilation of vital nourishment. The raw vegetable juices are digested within ten to fifteen minutes—the entire process of digestion is completed with a minimum of effort.

So, if you are fat or getting fat, take warning! Eat less and enjoy life—and sex—more.

15. Are You "Too Tired" for Sex?

FATIGUE IS ONE of the most potent warning signals that Nature has devised for unthinking human beings. Man has been trained to disregard fatigue, to ignore the warnings, to plunge bullheadedly along toward his goals. This is one reason why scores, if not hundreds of thousands, of misguided men and women live on the border line of nervous and physical collapse. They should recover with today's science and know-how!

When these misguided people break down from the accumulated results of fatigue, they blink in dazed fashion and look about for something or someone upon whom to hand the blame for their own dereliction. Yet the cause is usually plain—as simple as finding the answer to two plus two.

Just what is fatigue? What causes it? And what does it do to us? First, there is the chronic fatigue of many a person usually labeled a "Weary Willie" or a "Weary Wilhelmina." These worthies have an inherent disinclination toward exertion of any kind. Such apathy may be a state of mind. This form of fatigue is removed only by some great physical or spiritual regeneration.

Secondly, there is chemical fatigue, due to the accumulation of fatigue wastes or fatigue poisons in the system. This is a thoroughly normal condition when it doesn't go beyond normal bounds. Every living individual fortunate enough to earn this superb quality of fatigue is to be heartily congratulated. It is the soporific that brings the blessed sleep to heavy eyelids more effectively than anything that was ever poured out of a bottle, rolled in a pill, or squirted from a hypo.

Focal infections and toxins from decaying teeth and septic gums may be contributing causes to fatigue as are also the poisons absorbed by autointoxication resulting from constipation. Other frequent causes of fatigue are the excessive indulgence in stimulants, such as tea, coffee, cola drinks, or the direct action of narcotics such as headache powders, tobacco, and alcohol.

Then there is the fatigue that results from exhaustion of nerve force—the draining from nerve cells of their vital energy. This is the type of fatigue that brings about most of the "nervous breakdowns" of modern life and causes the vast increase in the army of neurasthenics.

To completely remove fatigue, and keep it removed, is a life time job with no vacations. It suggests that conserving nervous energy is a business of building nerve force and of scrupulously guarding the balance on the credit side.

Sexual intercourse is an intense act that completely controls the human body and the soul. Intercourse calls for muscular exertions that make demands on the nerves. After intercourse there is sudden relaxation. This sudden relaxation, after tension of a sharp nature, causes fatigue and sometimes a certain amount of exhaustion. A high degree of tension means a more sudden relaxation with consequent severity of fatigue and degree of exhaustion. Intercourse between lovers usually means a high degree of tension whereas coitus carried out quickly without the communion of intense rapture will lead to a lesser degree of fatigue Ecstasy in the woman recedes gradually so that a woman is much less fatigued than her male partner. For the man the sensation is usually a drowsy, dreamy one with the need for sleep sometimes becoming overpowering.

After intercourse the average person may need four or five minutes of repose before returning to a normal state. Many men promptly fall asleep after intercourse, especially if they are already fatigued and if the act occurs in the evening after a long day of work or play. Some few people may be fatigued for a few hours but these persons are usually in ill health or the cause may be due to late hours and lack of sleep.

Just as all people have a limit to the amount of physical strain they can bear, so also there is a limit on mental strain. This will react on a person's sex life. Sexual life depends on the mind. Tension, stress, bitterness, discontent, worry, and anxiety are enemies to a fulfilling sex life. The nervous system must not become charged with fear or apprehension. It is the ability of man to keep an even keel, to find solutions to his problems, and to see his own situations in perspective that contributes to a successful sexual union. The key to this is relaxation! Man and woman must acquire a tranquil, peaceful state of mind. This can be found by relying on inner sources.

Doctor Hans Selye has pointed out that physical or mental fatigue can diminish sexual desire. A person must be well-rested and have a sense of well-being to enjoy coitus completely. Daily annoyances and inconsequential physical aches and pains must not exclude the impulse for pleasure. Reproduction is not the sole purpose of the sexual act. Not only are normal sex relations a pleasure but they relieve tension.

Physical changes can result from emotional tension. The stomach can react to tension by secreting excessive amounts of acid. At first the symptoms will be cramps, hunger pains, or burning pains. If not controlled, in some instances this tension can create a sore that finally develops into an ulcer. Tension can cause a rapid heart, or an irregular heart, elevated blood pressure, tiredness, and many other symptoms in various parts of the body.

In this generation it seems imperative that men and women should learn how to relax. An ideal would be to practice the art of relaxation two or three times daily—each session for about fifteen or thirty minutes. Try to give yourself entirely over to the bed. By observing yourself you will see how continuously and strenuously you hold yourself in a certain position on the bed. You will find most of your muscles cramped, your head held rigidly in a certain position, your spinal column quite inflexible. You are doing hard muscular work and not relaxing

In addition to exerting physical tension when going to bed, many people begin to do strenuous mental work—thoughts stream through their mind in an unending procession. As there is a great riciprocal action between the mind and the body, it has been discovered that at times it is best to use the mind to concentrate on relaxing the body. Concentrating on body relaxation will release the person from nervous tension and at the same time the mind will be occupied with helpful work and not sleep-destroying useless worry.

In addition to the regular periods for relaxation and periods for rest following work or play there should be a lessening of the useless expenditure of energy in so many needless stress and strain situations encountered in our daily life.

Sexual intercourse does not weaken a man. It is relaxing. It dissipates nervous tension. Sexual intercourse a few hours before an athletic activity, such as golf, may prove beneficial. This can reduce any nervous tension present and induce a proper state of relaxation during the game.

On an average, most healthy grown persons require about eight to nine hours of sleep. Women should have half an hour or an hour more than men of the same age. There is a division of opinion about how much sleep is needed by a person over sixty. A man or woman past sixty in good health may not require more than eight or nine hours of restful sleep. When seventy or eighty, an afternoon nap of an hour does have beneficial effects. A rest from all activity following meals also serves to recharge the batteries in advanced age groups. For the retired person, often six hours of restful sleep will be sufficient. But a majority of scientists agree that chronic lack of sleep and rest can cause premature ageing.

A survey of physicians who had patients over sixty years of age with complaints ranging from tension to apprehension disclosed that many had sleep cycles of seven hours and less. The complaints of these people disappeared when their sleep was increased to nine or ten hours at night combined with a one hour nap in the afternoon. The nap also contributed to an improvement of the quality of the night's sleep.

If you are "too tired" for sex, get plenty of sleep and learn to relax.

16. How to Attract a Mate

WHAT IS IT that attracts a man to a particular woman or to some particular type of woman? Is it the color of her hair and her complexion? Is it because of her exquisite and refreshing cleanliness and scrupulous care of her person, her nails, and her skin? Is it because of her manner of dressing, ornamentation, or perfume? Is it her expression, demeanor, disposition, or character? Is it because she has intelligence or because she lacks it? Is it some subtle bond of sympathy that may exist? Or is it because she has learned the subtle art of flattery and of encouraging confidences?

Granted that complexion, color, clothes, and exquisite care of the body are vitally essential, and that sympathetic intelligence is a great asset, there is yet one quality even more important than any or all of these put together. This quality is *personal magnetism*, or personality.

If a woman has personal magnetism, she may sport a reasonable amount of freckles or a snub nose. She may dance as though she has two left feet. But she can't be sickly, sluggish, pimply, dry-haired, or scaly-skinned. She cannot have a disgusting breath, or a set of teeth that are a disgrace. In brief, she must radiate exuberant spirits, vitality, and vivacity. And she must be clean, sweet, and wholesome from hair to feet.

With good health, a clean wholesome body, and a vivacious spirit, a woman can attract almost any unattached normal healthy man that she wants to attract.

Perhaps the most important gland or glands that have to do with the beauty of a woman are the ovaries. It is the perfect functioning of these glands that gives to the woman her charm of femininity, her soft curves, her pitch of voice, and the comparative absence of hair upon the face, neck, and breast.

It is upon the proper functioning of the ovaries that the sweetness of disposition, too, largely depends. And upon this, as everyone knows, a definite part of the personality of an individual devolves. Almost everyone knows women who cannot by the widest stretch of the imagination be called beautiful, and yet there is something of an illusive charm about their eyes, about their gracious winning smile, and about their general demeanor that makes them seem comely despite a plain variety of features.

We are attracted to a mate because of certain erotically appealing qualities. The sex-appeal may differ among personalities. This may account for the phenomenon of what are considered strangely assorted couples—the short man who mates with a very tall woman, the tiny woman with a very tall man, the thin man with a very heavy woman, or the lean woman with an obese man. There is some erotic sex-appeal at work when man meets woman! Sex-appeal is at work in the man or woman after sixty when they meet and when they mate. It is a life-long quality!

Of the five senses, sight comes first in sexual attraction. The attraction through the sense of sight accounts for the great number and variety of beauty salons, barber shops, establishments for the sale of clothes to men and women—all to make customers more appealing through the sense of sight.

The ornamentation and clothes of women exert a sex-stimulating influence on men. It is also a fact that men, in their turn, through clothes and ornament, are not entirely devoid of certain stimulating influences upon women. This fact is emphasized by the almost universal infatuation exerted by the sight of a gaudy uniform, especially if decorated with a couple of rows of medals, a display of gold braid, and a glittering sword.

However, failing to secure a general or an admiral, many women are only too happy to receive the attentions of any wearer of a uniform, his rank, of course, being balanced against her station in life. This provides automatically for interest in soldiers, sailors, policemen, firemen, and uniformed employees of hotels and apartment houses. This provides the basis for the many separations between wives and their men in uniform. The disillusion that comes from seeing the man in civies can be too great, especially to couples with poor sex performance.

Some men are sexually attracted to women in uniform. Nurses in their freshly starched white uniforms can evoke erotic sensation as can the airline stewardess in her flashy outfit. A waitress, a saleswoman, or any woman in uniform will attract some men.

Whatever his age, a man should be dressed stylishly. So often the man who retires after sixty or sixty-five finds himself with a closet full of clothes, some hardly worn. No longer compelled to dress up for the office, he decides to wear out this supply of suits, shoes, and neckwear, with the result that soon he looks out of date. His age is accented. Some men react sharply when this is brought to their attention—they purchase clothes designed for the very young in an effort to appear less mature, and only lose their dignity, poise, and character in the process.

Women have always known the fascination exercised by dress and decoration. All the manifold absurdities in women's attire have been invented for the specific purpose of accenting certain sexual attributes. Today dress emphasizes the sexual attraction of the thighs; at one time it was the leg; at another time it was the breasts; at another the abdomen; and at another it was the buttocks. When a fashion becomes stale and no longer is the subject of conversation and attention, something new is introduced. This change of fashion extends to foot-wear and other accessories.

At night it is time for the theater and for the dance, a time of mutual attraction of the sexes. Female exposure of the body in the evening is always greater than in the day. Sex flourishes at night.

Long ago the women of Greece, Egypt, China, and India began using cosmetics—powder, rouge, lipstick, various creams, and dyes. Today's women are using the same articles, the same preparations—nothing is new except the names of the colors and of the scents! Although the color of the eyes cannot be changed, everything is done to accent their shape, change their form, color the lids, and extend the length of the lashes for just one purpose—sex attraction. Lip color is constantly being changed as is the color of rouge and powders. This is a tremendous industry basically geared to sex achievement.

It is only natural that a woman should make herself attractive, whatever her age. It is heartening to see so many women sixty and over take such an interest in their appearance—they do look many years younger than they are. They think young, which in turn makes them act young. It gives any woman a lift to be admired, to be complimented on her appearance.

Cosmetics should be used to enhance a woman's physical features and to detract from her poor features. They can be used to cover up minor blemishes and by artful application the entire face can be made more attractive. A woman can be sexually exciting with careful eye make-up, inviting lips, and a beautiful becoming skin tone—whatever her age!

In the sensation of seeing, color is paramount—the color of clothes, of hair, and of complexion. Red has come through the ages as the most popular color for both clothes and cosmetics—notice the vast number of red shades of lipstick and rouge!

Women change their hair color until they find one that they believe is sexually attractive. Changes in hair styles come and go—at one time the hair is straight, at another period it is curled, or it is piled high, or it is flat!

Hair is also important in enhancing the appearance of men. There are two things a man can do when he starts to become bald—he can do nothing and possibly lose all his hair, or he can acquire a false hair piece. Increasingly today men color their hair. Some must do so in order to hold a position. Some men apply hair color to impress a woman, to appear younger than they are. It also gives them a certain satisfaction—they enjoy being told that ten or twenty years has been removed from their actual age. However, many women only love a man with grey or white hair—they find these men exciting and appealing, a source of strength and security.

Second of the five senses in sex is hearing. Hearing can animate sexual fulfillment.

Hearing a person speak very loudly can dampen sexual appeal. This applies also to a person who speaks very softly—the listener who must strain to hear the words can lose interest in sexual thoughts. Speaking too fast or too slow will not add to sex encouragement. In addition there is the import of the words. They must be interesting. The very quality of a conversation can augment sexual achievement. This does not mean that a conversation should consist of off-color jokes or anecdotes or the detailing of indecent or pornographic stories.

It is the tone of the voice that is all important. The person with a high-pitched screeching sound will grate on the eardrums. This reacts on the sexual organs and can inhibit sexual activity. A man or a woman's voice can have a pronounced erotic quality—soft and soothing. The actor and the singer work diligently to cultivate a pleasing voice with one thought in mind—to appeal to our sense of hearing. Who can enjoy sexual intercourse with discordant music being played fortissimo in the next room or with the street outside the window being torn up by a powerful bulldozer?

Many men and women of mature age have learned to moderate their voices, to use their lower more pleasing tones. They cultivate a more sexy voice!

In music it has been found that certain rhythms can produce physiologic effects in a sexual manner. The production of sounds in music, the manner in which music is performed, either vocally or by instrument, can often start erotic feelings. Sensual, dreamy combinations of sounds can inflame the libido. Dreary, gloomy music can produce sadness and melancholy that can extinguish sexual ardor. Changes in the volume of music, unexpected sharp sounds, changes in tempo, and the repetitions of sounds can influence sexual desire. In more primitive people the continuous beat of the drums or tom-tom can rouse dormant desire.

Third of the five senses in sex is that of touch. It is tactile contact that often brings on sexual response. The sense of touch is predominant in love play—petting, kissing, and stroking. Sexual response begins through the end organs of touch—the nerve endings. These are located in the skin and in some of the deeper nerves of the body. There are certain areas of the body that are richly supplied with end organs and have been classified as *erogenous zones*. These areas are recognized in the petting techniques of both men and women.

By touch the erogenous zones can be sufficiently stimulated to cause orgasm in some people. This contradicts the widely held belief that only through stimulation of the genitalia can arousal of this magnitude be achieved. The hand is the principal tactile agent—the fingers and tips of the fingers. The tongue and the lips are next in importance.

Some zones are more easily stimulated than others. The mouth, the lips, and the nose are highly erogenous zones. The lobe and helix of the ear, the nape of the neck, and the nipples are highly susceptible to the sense of touch. The man and woman over sixty will always continue to enjoy touching the erogenous zones of their mate—arousing desire by the sense of touch!

The sense of smell—odors—have been used extensively as an allurement, enticement, and temptation. The Egyptian woman of three thousand years ago understood the erotic attraction to be found in the scent of henna. Musk was a decided sexual stimulant from that period to the present. The popularity of perfume among women has never diminished. It is probable that strong odors and spices have direct effect upon the nervous system and can start the physiologic changes that constitute sexual response.

Women seem more susceptible to the sense of smell than men. Their ability to distinguish a range of personal odors is greater than in men. The perfumer is not insensitive to these facts, as witness the great quantities of perfumes being placed on the market for men—all kinds of fragrant toilet preparations, shaving soap, hair and mouth washes, body preparations, and face creams labeled as an allure for women—all guaranteed to capture by that "manly" smell.

Many people are conscious of the fact that they are sexually stimulated by things that they smell. There are people whose sense of smell is highly developed. There are other people that have little or no response to pleasant or unpleasant odors.

People differ in their personal individual odor. This does not mean the odor of perspiration or of an unclean body or from clothing. It means that everyone has an individual odor. A dog recognizes his master by his individual smell, not by sight.

Normal genital odors do attract a person of the opposite sex. There is a distinctive sexual odor from these organs. It is not pronounced as a rule and usually cannot be perceived until a couple has coitus or considerable intimacy. This genital odor is more powerful in the female—especially so when the female is aroused and ready for coitus. Faint and often unnoticed by the male, this odor acts as a special enticement!

There is no evidence to show any decline in sensory perception for the man and woman over sixty. So remember the senses as you set about attracting a mate.